contents

foreword

Learning to become clean and dry is an important step in your child's journey towards independence – but he'll need lots of help from you along the way. There are many possible ways to potty train your child, and it can often seem that everyone you speak to has a different opinion about the best way to go about it. Like other aspects of baby care there are fads that become popular with one generation of parents only to be discounted by the next. One thing is certain: whether you start sitting your baby on a potty at a few months old or wait until your child is able to understand and communicate his needs, the end result will be the same – however you choose to get there.

This book gives you a complete guide to this vital period of your child's life. Inside, you'll find everything you need to understand how your baby's 'waste disposal' system works – and what can go wrong with it – together with guidance on how best to take care of your child's bottom. The book explains all the different approaches to potty training, how to know when your toddler is ready to begin and how to go about preparing for it all. And when you begin the training itself, you'll find plenty of clear, helpful advice to guide you along each step of the way, showing how to make this a fun and exciting time for you and your child to enjoy.

1 How it all works

To understand how your child learns to recognize and then control his need to pass urine or have a bowel movement, it helps to know exactly how the body systems that are responsible for these functions work. And since the proper development and functioning of the urinary and digestive systems is so essential to your child's health and happiness – in addition to making your own life a great deal more pleasant – it also helps to understand just what can go wrong with them.

the urinary system

The organs in your child's urinary system, or urinary tract, are responsible for filtering the blood to remove excess water and unwanted material, and then excreting it as urine, or pee. Urine is produced in your child's kidneys and then transferred to his bladder through the ureters, the tubes that connect the kidneys to the bladder. The bladder is a balloon-like muscle that stretches as it fills with urine. The bottom, or neck, of the bladder is kept closed by a circular group of muscles called the urethral sphincter. This automatically stays contracted to hold in the urine until your child's bladder is full.

During the early months of life, your baby's bladder only holds a very small amount of urine. As soon as the bladder is full, it automatically contracts and empties, forcing urine down the urethra, which leads to the vulva in girls and the penis in boys. As your baby grows, the capacity of the bladder will increase. By the time he has reached toddlerhood, voluntary control of the sphincter muscles will start to develop, and you will notice that your child passes urine less frequently. This is just one of the signs that your child is ready to begin potty training.

How much and how often?

Your baby has no control over his bladder during the early weeks of life, so he may wet his nappy as frequently as 20 times in 24 hours. Once feeding is established, he can produce as much as 200 ml (⅓ pint) of urine in that time, even at a very early age. This may seem like a lot when you are constantly changing wet nappies, until

Although young babies have no control over their bladders, they sometimes pick the most inopportune moments to let it all out. Baby boys, especially, are often stimulated to urinate by the feeling of cold air on their skin – so watch out at nappy-changing time!

important to increase your child's fluid intake by increasing his feeds and offering cooled, boiled water in between meals. You can give an older baby or toddler extra drinks of diluted fruit juice or normal tap water.

What colour is normal?

Healthy urine is straw coloured, however it is quite normal for the nappy of your newborn to be stained dark pink or even red. This is because a newborn's urine contains substances called urates, waste products present in his blood at birth. This discoloration will disappear within a few days. If your baby is a girl, there may be some slight bleeding from the vagina, which can make her urine appear discoloured, but this is quite normal during the first few days.

In an older baby or toddler, urine can become discoloured through drinking blackcurrant juice or similar dark-coloured liquids. If, however, you suspect the discoloration is caused by blood in the urine you should consult your doctor

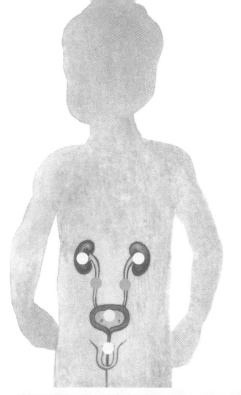

THE URINARY SYSTEM

kidneys   bladder

ureters   urethra

you compare it with an adult who, with bladder control, only needs to pee around six times during the same period, even though his body is producing about 1½ litres (3 pints) of urine.

As your baby gets older and the capacity of his bladder increases, you will notice that the frequency with which he wets his nappy lessens. However, your baby should still pass urine every few hours. If he doesn't it could be because he is not be getting enough fluid, or he may be losing fluid through sweating or through being bundled up in too many clothes. If your child is ill and has a fever, he will use up extra fluid, which will also affect the amount of urine he produces. Lack of fluid can lead to dehydration, which can be dangerous in babies and young children, so it is

IS YOUR CHILD DEHYDRATED?

It is not necessary for your child to drink constantly, but it is important that she maintains a regular fluid intake through the day. A simple way to check if your child has drunk enough is to check the colour of her urine. As a rule of thumb, the paler the urine, the better.

If your child seems dehydrated, give her plenty of clear fluids (cooled, boiled water for young babies). If severely dehydrated, your child should receive urgent medical attention.

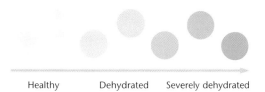

Healthy   Dehydrated   Severely dehydrated

 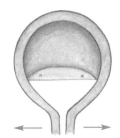 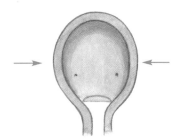

As the bladder fills, sphincter muscles at the neck prevent urine leaking out. At the same time, stretch receptors trigger the urge to urinate.

When the bladder is full, the muscles relax to let out urine. In young children this process is automatic, but older children develop voluntary control.

As the sphincter muscles relax, muscles in the wall of the bladder contract, forcing urine out of the bladder, down the urethra and out of the body.

immediately, as this may indicate some type of urinary tract infection or a problem such as glomerulonephritis (see p.9). Urine that appears dark yellow and concentrated means that your child is not getting enough fluid and you will need to make sure he gets more to drink.

How should pee smell?

Normal pee has practically no smell, so any unusual smell could be a sign that something is wrong. Pee that appears strongly concentrated and has an unusual odour could indicate that your child has a urinary tract infection.

If you smell ammonia when you change a nappy, this usually means the nappy isn't being changed frequently enough. Ammonia is produced when bacteria in faeces react with the urine in a wet nappy, and is a powerful irritant that frequently causes nappy rash. You are more likely to encounter this problem if you use cloth nappies, because most disposables are designed to draw urine away from the skin. Also, if you are breast-feeding there is less likelihood of this happening, as the composition of breast milk makes a child's urine more acidic and this will discourage bacteria.

What can go wrong

Occasionally, children are born with physical defects of the urinary tract. These are usually identified soon after birth and in most cases can be treated before the child reaches school age. More common are infections affecting the urinary tract. These always need medical attention, as left untreated they risk damaging the organs in your child's urinary system.

Hypospadias

This is a congenital abnormality which occurs in around 1 in 300 boys. Boys with hypospadias have the opening of their urethra, the tube from which urine leaves the body, on the underside of the penis rather than at the tip. Because it is not possible for them to produce a normal stream of urine, surgery to extend the urethra is usually carried out before the age of two. After surgery, urine can be passed quite normally.

Urinary reflux

Very occasionally, an abnormality of a child's ureters – the tubes that join the kidneys to the bladder – causes small amounts of urine to flow back up the ureters when the bladder is emptied.

This can lead to urinary infections in babies and young children. The problem often disappears without treatment as the body matures, but if you think your child may have the condition you must consult your doctor or healthcare provider.

Urinary tract infections

These are a serious but common health problem in babies and young children, and always require medical treatment because of the risk of kidney damage. Urinary tract infections (UTIs) are caused when bacteria, usually E. coli from the bowel, multiply around the opening of your child's urethra. If the infection is limited to the urethra it is called urethritis. Very often the bacteria move up to the bladder causing cystitis, a bladder infection. If the infection is not treated properly, bacteria may then spread to the kidneys causing pyelonephritis, a kidney infection.

It is estimated that around 3 per cent of girls and 1 per cent of boys will have had a UTI by the age of 11. Girls are more prone to UTIs because the way their genitalia is arranged means the urethra can come into contact with bowel movements more easily. Another factor is that the urethra is much shorter in girls than in boys, which makes it easier for bacteria to spread upward. Some children are more prone to getting urinary tract infections than others. See p.30 for advice on symptoms and treatment.

Glomerulonephritis

This is an inflammation of the filtering units in the kidneys, the glomeruli, which means they are not able to process waste efficiently. The amount of urine produced is reduced, and blood and protein give it a red, pink or smoky colour. Glomerulonephritis sometimes occurs as a result of an infection by streptococcal bacteria or by viruses. Treatment is usually in hospital, where your child may be given a low sodium and protein diet to prevent strain being put on the kidneys. If the infection is caused by bacteria, antibiotics will be given. With treatment, glomerulonephritis usually clears up within a week with no lasting effect on the kidneys.

URINE OUTPUT AT DIFFERENT AGES

Young babies produce much less urine than older children over the course of a day. But because their bladders are so much smaller, and the process of urination is automatic, they pee far more frequently – as anyone who has to change wet nappies will certainly testify!

Age	Output per day
0 to 48 hours	15 to 60 ml
3 to 10 days	100 to 300 ml
10 to 60 days	250 to 450 ml
2 to 12 months	400 to 500 ml
1 to 3 years	500 to 600 ml
3 to 5 years	600 to 700 ml
5 to 8 years	650 to 1000 ml
8 to 14 years	800 to 1400 ml

the digestive system

The role of your child's digestive system is essentially twofold: to break down food so that the body can absorb its nutrients into the bloodstream, and to eliminate waste in the form of faeces (also known as stools, a movement or poop). A properly functioning system is essential for your child's health and well-being – and will make life much easier for you too.

Digestion

The digestive system can be thought of as one long tube, running from the mouth down to the anus, and the food your child eats will pass through many distinct stages along the way.

The process begins in your child's mouth, when food first enters the body and is chewed and swallowed. Already, enzymes in your child's saliva are working to break down starchy foods. This mash is then carried down the oesophagus and into your child's stomach by the wave-like contraction of muscles known as peristalsis. This is usually a one-way process, but occasionally food can travel in the other direction – when your child vomits, food is forcibly ejected from the stomach and back up the oesophagus. This is an important way for your child's body to remove dangerous substances before they can be absorbed into the bloodstream.

Even though your baby may only be having a small amount of solids each day, you may notice that the consistency of his stools change to become more formed.

YOUR CHILD'S DIGESTIVE SYSTEM

Food is propelled along your child's digestive system (*far right*) by the coordinated relaxation and contraction of muscles (*right*), a process known as peristalsis.

- mouth
- oesophagus
- stomach
- small intestine
- large intestine
- rectum

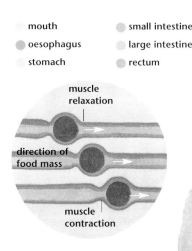

muscle relaxation

direction of food mass

muscle contraction

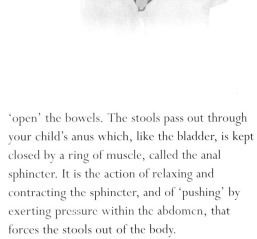

In the stomach, the food is broken down further as it is churned and kneaded by the stomach muscles and mixed with gastric juices. These acidic juices break down all but the toughest components and provide a vital defence against germs. But it is in the long, winding small intestine that most of the actual absorption of the nutrients occurs. These nutrients provide the fuel that powers your child's body as it develops and keeps her healthy.

Finally, any waste matter that remains ends up in your child's bowel, which is a part of the large intestine. Here, excess water is reabsorbed, leaving a semi-solid mass – the faeces.

Excretion

Your child's faeces contain the indigestible parts of the food your child eats, such as fibre, as well as the waste products of normal bodily processes and any toxic substances that the body wishes to remove. Bile pigments lend the stool its colour, and nitrogen compounds, produced by the action of bacteria, give its characteristic odour.

From the bowel, this faecal matter is passed to the rectum, where it is stored. Once the rectum is full, pressure from within produces the urge to 'open' the bowels. The stools pass out through your child's anus which, like the bladder, is kept closed by a ring of muscle, called the anal sphincter. It is the action of relaxing and contracting the sphincter, and of 'pushing' by exerting pressure within the abdomen, that forces the stools out of the body.

As with the bladder, this happens automatically until your toddler has developed sufficiently to gain voluntary control of these muscles.

A mother's breast milk is very easy for babies to digest and contains antibodies that can help prevent infections. As a result, breast-fed babies are less likely than those fed on formula milk to suffer from digestive problems such as constipation or diarrhoea.

How much and how often?

There is no such thing as a 'normal' number of stools, or a correct number of times your child should pass them. What is normal for one child may be completely different for another. Some newborn babies have a bowel movement each time they feed because the action of sucking and swallowing sets off the reflex that opens the anal sphincter. Others, usually those who are being breast-fed, may be well and content going for several days without passing a stool. The reason for this is thought to be that your breast milk is so perfectly matched to your baby's needs that there is hardly any waste material to pass out as stools. If your baby is fed formula milk she is likely to pass stools fairly regularly, usually around once or twice a day. However, as with breast-fed babies, more or less than this is also perfectly normal, as long as the stools, when they do come, are soft and easy to pass.

A toddler, eating a normal diet, may pass stools once or twice a day, others may need to go every other day. Less often than this is also normal and as long as the stools are not hard and your child has no difficulty in passing them, this is not anything to be concerned about. Some children have a natural tendency towards constipation and can be affected, not only by diet or lack of fluid, but also by upsets or changes in routine. If your child has a tendency toward constipation ask your doctor or healthcare provider for advice. Never be tempted to give your child any laxatives or suppositories unless they have been prescribed by your doctor.

What colour and consistency?

Your baby's first stools will be a blackish-green colour as the meconium from the amniotic fluid works its way out of her system. Once feeding is established, her stools will become loose and yellow if she is breast-fed, or browner and firmer if she is having formula milk. Changing from one type of formula to another may result in runny stools for a few days, until your baby is used to the new feed. If these runny stools last for more than four days you should ask your doctor for advice. Breast-fed babies are unlikely to have diarrhoea, but if it occurs, particularly if accompanied by vomiting, fever or blood in the stools, you should consult your doctor or healthcare provider immediately.

Once you start weaning your baby, you may notice that the colour and consistency of her stools change again. Introducing new foods, for example blackcurrant or beetroot, into the diet can produce what may seem like alarming colour changes in the stools, but this is quite normal.

What can go wrong

Sometimes, problems with your child's digestive system are caused by physical abnormalities within the digestive tract that are present at birth (congenital), and these may require surgical treatment. Occasional problems are much more likely to be due to an infection or to the introduction of new foods into your child's diet. Sometimes they are a sign of some underlying disorder, so persistent problems should always be checked by your doctor or healthcare provider.

Hirschsprung's disease (HD)

This is a rare disease of the large intestine, which develops before a child is born. The nerve cells that are responsible for making the muscles 'push' are missing in the last part of the large intestine. This results in a build-up of stools, causing very bad constipation. In extreme cases, the disease may prevent the child from having a bowel movement at all. Treatment is with surgery, and if successful the child will be able to have normal bowel movements.

Intestinal obstruction

In some cases, bowel problems can be caused by an intestinal obstruction, which leads to a partial or complete blockage. This may be due to a congenital abnormality of the intestine, or to an acquired problem, such as a strangulated hernia. This type of hernia occurs when a section of the intestine protrudes through the abdominal wall, preventing the passage of food and obstructing the blood supply to the protruding section.

In children under two, an obstruction may be caused by a disorder known as intussusception, where part of the intestine telescopes in on itself, usually where the small intestine meets the large intestine. A child with an intestinal obstruction usually requires surgery, although in the case of intussusception a barium or air enema may be given to force the intestine back into the right position.

INTUSSUSCEPTION

Cross-section of intestine

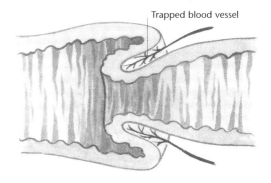

Trapped blood vessel

Intussusception occurs when one portion of the intestine slips inside another. This obstructs the regular passage of matter through your child's system, and can cut off the blood supply to any blood vessels trapped between the two segments. It should therefore be treated urgently.

Lack of fluid is a common cause of constipation, so you should make sure your child always has plenty to drink.

Constipation

This is when a child has dry, hard stools that are difficult to pass. Infrequent bowel movements are not necessarily a sign of constipation – some breast-fed babies go for several days between stools, but as long as the stools are soft and easy to pass this is nothing to worry about.

Constipation is not itself a disease. Rather, it is a symptom of problems with the normal working of your child's digestion, meaning your child finds it difficult or painful to expel the stools that have formed. There may be too little water in the stools, making them dry and difficult to pass – dehydration is a very common cause of constipation and babies who are bottle-fed may have problems if their feeds are incorrectly mixed. Also, although babies and toddlers do not need a high-fibre diet, lack of fibre can cause constipation. Fibre holds water, making the stools softer, and adds bulk, making them easier to pass. Other factors, such as stress or upsets, can sometimes cause toddlers to physically hold in their stools. If you think your baby may be constipated you should always seek medical advice. See p.32 for more information about the treatment of constipation.

CHARLIE'S CONSTIPATION

Charlie had always been irregular, sometimes going up to three or four days between poops. I didn't worry at first because everyone told me this was quite normal. But when he became a toddler, his constipation became more of a problem and he developed an anal fissure. Then we got into a vicious circle – he wouldn't go because it hurt and the more he didn't go the more distressed and uncomfortable he became. I seemed to be spending half my life at the doctor's office getting prescriptions for suppositories, stool softeners and mild laxatives. At one point things had got so bad that he had to go into hospital to have an enema. He's four now and still does a poop only every couple of days, but at least he seems to have got over his bout of constipation.

Spastic constipation

This type of constipation is caused by the large intestine going into spasm and holding onto small pieces of the faeces until they become dried into little balls. The stools eventually appear as a collection of small, hard balls that are difficult to pass. Spastic constipation occurs only in children on a formula or solid-food diet. Sometimes the condition can be cured by making changes to your child's diet, but you should seek medical advice if you are concerned.

Anal fissure

Constipation makes the stools hard, and passing them may cause a small tear, known as an anal fissure, in the delicate mucous membrane of your child's anus. This makes it painful for your child to pass a stool and can lead to a small amount of bleeding from her anus. Although on first sight this is worrying, the bleeding is not usually serious – it is just like any bleeding from a small cut. There is a risk that a child with an anal fissure may try to avoid passing stools because of the pain, which can compound the problem by making the stools harder and even more difficult to pass. Drinking plenty of fluids will help keep stools soft and easy to pass. As the area is always moist, healing can take time.

Diarrhoea

This occurs when the lining of your child's intestine is irritated or injured, and water is not reabsorbed from the stool before being passed out of the body. The passing of a few extra stools that are looser than normal is quite common in young children because their intestine can be easily upset by germs or new foods. The stools may look greenish or smell offensive. As long as your child is otherwise healthy, peeing normally, and the diarrhoea doesn't last more than a couple of days, this is nothing to worry about.

Severe diarrhoea occurs when your child passes frequent, watery stools. If this lasts for more than a couple of days and is accompanied by vomiting and fever, it may be caused by an infection elsewhere in her body and will need medical treatment. Another possibility is that your child has a problem digesting certain types of foods, such as gluten (the protein found in wheat) or some types of sugars. Sometimes, an occasional bout of diarrhoea is caused by taking antibiotics. See p.31 for more information on the treatment of diarrhoea.

Toddler diarrhoea

From the end of the first year up to the age of two to three, the most common form of chronic (meaning longlasting or recurring) diarrhoea is called toddler diarrhoea. This is a non-specific

WATCH **POINT...**

Abdominal pain is very common in young children, but most tummy aches are fortunately not serious and tend to disappear on their own. If your child's tummy ache is accompanied by any of the following symptoms, however, you should always have it checked out by a doctor or other healthcare provider:

- High fever or a racing pulse

- Lack of energy or listlessness

- Unusual lack of appetite

- Tender-to-the-touch abdomen

- Pain that continues or worsens over a period of several hours

- Pain going to the toilet, vomiting, diarrhoea, constipation or abdominal swelling

TUMMY ACHE

" BARNEY'S DIARRHOEA

I had never heard of toddler diarrhoea until Barney was 18 months old. He was always quite prolific in that department and would do four or five poops a day, then at 16 months his bowel movements became explosive! I always had to take spare clothes with me when we went out because his nappy just couldn't contain the amount of poop he produced. He was perfectly well and healthy, and all the tests he had came back normal. In the end toddler diarrhoea was diagnosed. I started potty training him when he was two-and-a-half and he was dry quite quickly, but it took longer to get him clean because of the diarrhoea. He grew out of it eventually, but even now, at the age of five, he still tends to poop a couple of times a day.

"

form of diarrhoea, with no obvious medical cause, and is thought to occur because of an exaggerated reflex between the stomach and the bowel. This may be triggered by large meals, frequent snacks and cold drinks – especially fruit juice. If your child appears to be well and happy, with a good appetite and normal weight gain, there is nothing more to worry about than frequent, smelly nappies. Although it will wear off in time, this form of diarrhoea can make catching a bowel movement in the potty during potty training rather a challenge.

Gastroenteritis

This is a serious condition caused by a virus or bacteria, and may be the result of food poisoning. The bowel becomes irritated and inflamed, which causes frequent runny stools accompanied by abdominal pain, vomiting and fever. Diarrhoea and vomiting can quickly lead to dehydration, which can be dangerous in a young baby or child, so you should always seek immediate medical advice. For serious, bacterial gastroenteritis your doctor may feel antibiotics are needed, but this will not help viral infections. Indeed, antibiotics may aggravate the diarrhoea.

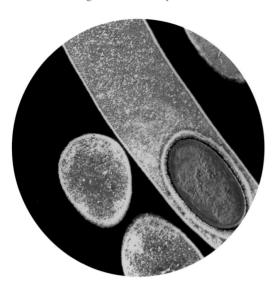

These *Clostridium* bacteria are one of many species of micro-organism that can cause gastroenteritis.

2 Taking care of your baby's bottom

Situated as it is at the end of such a highly efficient waste disposal system, it will come as no surprise that your baby's bottom is a high-maintenance area. During the first few years of life your baby will spend a great deal of time in nappies, and you'll need to work hard to make sure his bottom stays healthy, clean and dry. And when problems do occur, from constipation to nappy rash, you'll want to know how best to deal with them, keeping your baby as comfortable as possible.

choosing the right nappy

Nappies are going to play a big part in your life over the next few years, so it is important to choose the right type to suit both your lifestyle and your baby. Although they come in a wide variety of types, styles and sizes, the basic choice is between disposables and washables.

Disposables are certainly more convenient than washable cloth nappies, which need to be rinsed, sterilized, washed and dried. But because they can't be reused, they are likely to work out as more expensive in the long term. Many parents also feel that throwing a nappy into the bin each time they change their baby is far too wasteful.

Whatever your preference, there is no reason why you shouldn't be flexible. You may find that a combination of the two works best for you – cloth nappies at home, for example, and disposables while you are out and about.

Disposable nappies

These work by allowing moisture to soak through a top sheet into a moisture-absorbing gel, which soaks up the urine and keeps your baby's skin dry. Some nappies for newborns even draw liquid poop into the nappy. Disposables

Between birth and being potty trained, your baby is likely to have around 6,000 nappy changes. You won't always be delighted your baby's bowels are so prolific, but changing his nappies will give you both a chance to really get to know and get close to one another.

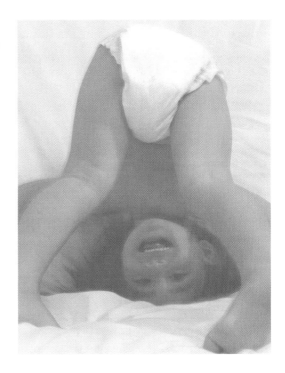

Advances in nappy technology mean that modern disposables are extremely absorbent, and fit well enough for even the most active baby.

come in a variety of shapes and sizes, with elasticated waists and legs, and protective waterproof backings. Some have lotion impregnated into them to help prevent nappy rash. They are held together with reusable tapes, which allow you to check whether your baby is dry. Even though they are very absorbent, they still need changing regularly.

Disposables are unisex, as their absorbency means that you don't need different styles for boys and girls. Some newborn nappies are made from a softer material than those for older babies, where a slimmer fit to go under clothes

NAPPY CHOICES

While I was pregnant with my first child, I decided that I would use cloth nappies and a laundry service – I was concerned about the sheer number of disposable nappies my baby would get through and the effect all those rotting nappies would have on the environment. But after only two months I gave up and changed to disposables. Although the nappy service was great, it was expensive and I still had to rinse and sterilize the nappies before they were collected. Although I do feel a bit guilty, disposables are just so much easier.

and stretchiness for an active baby are needed. You may need to try out several different brands before you find one that best suits your baby.

Disposing of your disposables

If you use disposables, you may find that your newborn needs as many as 12 a day. This drops to around seven a day during the first year, and then around five a day as he gets older – still a considerable amount. Although there is no doubt that disposables are more convenient than washable nappies, using this many will be expensive and, despite their name, they are not as easy to dispose of as they may sound. Most disposables end up being wrapped, or put in special plastic bags that neutralize strong odours, and placed in the rubbish bin. Alternatively, there are a number of portable units available that will wrap and seal the dirty nappy in strong film so that they can be stored in the unit for several days before being disposed of in bulk.

Washable nappies

A huge variety of cloth nappies are now available, from the simple terry-cotton squares to shaped all-in-ones with absorbent inner layers and waterproof outer covers. New materials and high-tech fabrics offer today's parents a wide range of choice – many of the technological advances offered by disposable manufacturers can now be found in cloth nappies, too. Unlike the disposables, however, these nappies can be used again and again. Washable nappies fall into three basic categories: traditional cloth squares, pre-shaped nappies and all-in-ones.

Traditional fabric squares

The more traditional cloth nappies come as a square that you can fold in a number of different ways to suit the shape and size of your baby. These are usually the least expensive type of nappy and dry very quickly. Because they are so easily adjustable, they usually give a very good fit.

The nappies are held together with pins, specially designed clips or special wraps. The cloth used for these nappies comes in a variety of absorbencies and qualities, and as a general guide the more absorbent the nappy the more expensive it is, so buy the best you can afford.

THE **NATURAL** APPROACH

It is a good idea to pre-wash new fabric nappies before putting them on your baby. Always avoid using standard detergents and bleach, as these can irritate your baby's sensitive skin. Some fabric conditioners will make nappies less absorbent, so you may prefer to use the old-fashioned alternative of adding half a cup of white vinegar to the final rinse instead.

WASHING ROUTINES

I used pre-shaped cloth nappies with all three of my children. Once I'd got into the routine of rinsing and sterilizing there was nothing to it. I washed the nappies every second day in the washing machine and dried them outside or in the tumble dryer. The nappies fit as well as disposables and cost a lot less money.

Pre-shaped nappies

These nappies come already tailored to fit babies' bottoms, so that it's no longer necessary to master all the intricacies of folding and pinning. Most have elasticated legs and waist, as well as Velcro fixings or poppers to keep them in place. Pre-shaped nappies are usually worn with a separate waterproof cover.

All-in-one nappies

Some top-of-the-range nappies make the job even easier for busy parents, with everything built-in. These nappies are shaped like regular disposables with an inner absorbent layer, Velcro or snap-type fastenings, elasticated legs and a built-in waterproof cover. They are as convenient and easy-to-use as disposable nappies, but when they're wet or dirty you can toss them into a nappy bucket instead of the rubbish bin.

Bear in mind, however, that your baby will grow very quickly – for comfort, adjustability and optimum containment it is difficult to beat a well-folded cloth square.

Extra costs

Washable nappies have the advantage of being a once-only buy, which makes them less expensive than disposables, although you do have to add in the cost of sterilizing and laundering them. If you use washable nappies you will need around 20 to 24 nappies, and you may also need pins or clips, biodegradable nappy liners, absorbent disposable pads and protective covers, depending on the style of nappy you choose. All cloth nappies need to be sterilized after use, so you will need a couple of nappy buckets, preferably with lids, and some sterilizing solution.

Liners

Using a biodegradable liner between the nappy and your baby's skin will enable you to flush the liner, along with any poop, straight down the toilet. The liner will also help to prevent the nappy from becoming stained. Once the liner is removed, any remaining soiling can usually be washed away with running water. If the nappy is just wet, the liner can simply be thrown away with your household rubbish.

Some biodegradable liners can be washed and dried, so liners that have only become wet can be reused a number of times.

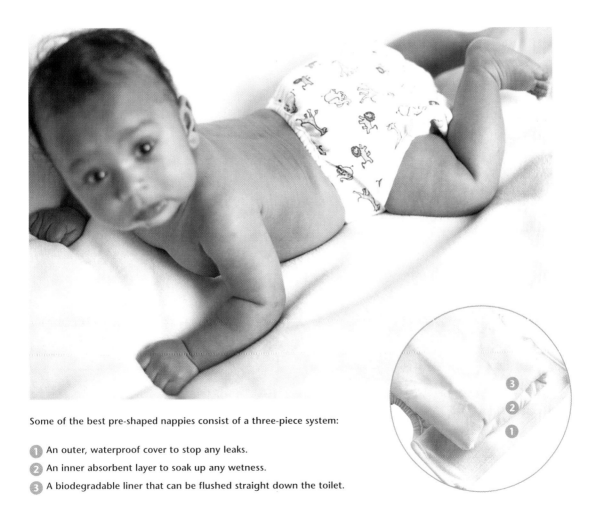

Some of the best pre-shaped nappies consist of a three-piece system:

1 An outer, waterproof cover to stop any leaks.

2 An inner absorbent layer to soak up any wetness.

3 A biodegradable liner that can be flushed straight down the toilet.

Caring for washable nappies

The days of having to boil nappies are long gone. Indeed boil-washing nappies may reduce the effectiveness of the nappies if it is done frequently. Check the washing instructions when you first buy your nappies as you'll find that different nappies have different maximum washing temperatures. For most nappies, a 60°C (140°F) wash is adequate, but there are some where 95°C (200°F) is suggested.

Sterilizing

Used nappies need to be sterilized in a nappy bucket before they are washed (see box, right). You can do this with one of the brand-name solutions available, although some of these may affect the elastic in pre-shaped nappies so check the care instructions on the nappy first. For a natural alternative to these solutions, see the box, below. Whatever type you use, you will need to make a fresh batch of solution each day.

Rinsing and washing

You may want to wash the nappies every day, or it may be more convenient to wait until you have a couple of days worth of used nappies to wash.

After sterilizing, drain off the excess liquid and, using a pair of rubber gloves, place the nappies in the washing machine on their own. Start with a pre-wash or short rinse and spin

THE **NATURAL** APPROACH

Instead of using harsh, brand-name sterilizing solutions, why not opt for a natural alternative? Adding two to three tablespoons of white distilled vinegar, or five drops of tea tree oil, to an average-size bucket of water will make an effective, eco-friendly solution.

cycle to rinse the nappies with fresh water, before washing them at the recommended temperature. Some proprietary sterilizing solutions may not require the nappies to be washed with detergent after rinsing, so check the manufacturer's instructions first.

Drying

Sunshine will naturally dry and bleach nappies, so whenever possible dry the nappies outdoors. If you have to dry them indoors, hang them on a clothes line or airer, as radiators may make them hard and uncomfortable. Most nappies can be tumble dried, which will help keep them soft.

Plastic pants

If you use plastic pants over the top of the fabric nappy, wash them in warm water with a little washing-up liquid. Tumble dry on a low heat to prevent the plastic becoming brittle, or hang them to dry. Try not to let the plastic come into contact with nappy creams and ointments.

Nappy laundry services

Parents who find the idea of all this washing and drying a little daunting may prefer to make use of a local nappy laundry service. The additional cost of this service, especially if you own your own washing machine, may be a consideration, but there is no doubt they offer significant advantages to busy parents. There is also a possible ecological advantage to using a nappy laundry service – by washing a large number of nappies together, it saves on the amount of electricity and water used. And the satisfaction of receiving a twice-weekly delivery of soft, clean, freshly laundered nappies should certainly not be underestimated.

Sterilizing, washing and drying your baby's nappies can be a very time-consuming process, so make sure you have everything you need for the job ready before you begin. Soiled nappies should be sterilized in a different bucket to nappies that are wet with urine, so it is a good idea to have different coloured buckets, so they are easy to tell apart.

1 Using a pair of rubber gloves, make up enough sterilizing solution in a bucket to completely cover the nappies you will be sterilizing. Make sure that the solution is always kept well out of reach of children.

2 After rinsing or scraping the worst of the soiling off the nappies, submerge in the sterilizing solution. Leave to soak for at least six hours.

3 Use a pair of tongs to remove the nappies from the sterilizing solution. Drain off the solution and, using the rubber gloves, place the nappies into the washing machine.

Environmental issues

A great deal of research has been done on the environmental impact of nappies, but as most has been done by disposable manufacturers or groups promoting washables, it is not generally unbiased.

Washables

Although the material these are made from is considered more eco-friendly than disposables, washing cloth nappies uses electricity, water and detergent – all of which have an impact on the environment. This can be reduced by using a nappy laundry service (see p.22).

Disposables

Over 90 per cent of disposables end up in landfill sites, and it is estimated that some parts of the nappies take up to 500 years to decompose completely. Most disposables contain paper pulp, absorbent gel, plastics and chemical additives, all of which affect the environment – paper pulp produces carbon dioxide and methane as it decays. In response to these concerns there are now a number of eco-friendly disposables available, designed to break down more quickly and using less chemical gels and bleaches, although these do tend to be more expensive than regular nappies.

nappy changing procedures

Whichever type of nappy you are using, your baby should be changed whenever she is wet or dirty so that her skin does not come into prolonged contact with urine or faeces. The number of times your baby will need changing may vary from day to day, but as a general guide you will need to change her when she first wakes in the morning, after each feeding, after a bath and before bed at night.

Before you begin, get everything you are going to need together, so that there is no reason to leave your baby during the time you are changing her. Place a folded towel or changing mat on the floor or the bed, or if you are using a changing unit place your baby on the unit's changing surface using the integral safety harness, if there is one. Do remember that there is always a risk that a wriggling baby could roll off a raised surface so she should never be left unattended.

Cleaning your baby

Before changing the nappy, always clean the nappy area thoroughly to prevent urine or faeces remaining on your child's skin and causing irritation. Rather than using soaps or bath detergents, which can irritate or dry out your baby's sensitive skin, use a baby wipe, or cotton wool with baby lotion or water.

Try to get everyone in the family involved in changing the baby's nappies – this is an excellent opportunity to really bond with your baby.

CLEANING YOUR BABY

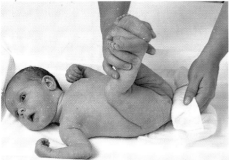

1 As you remove your baby's nappy, use a clean corner to wipe away the worst of any mess. Then, gently but firmly, hold your baby's legs down on the changing mat and use a baby wipe or moistened ball of cotton wool to clean around her tummy.

2 Using a fresh wipe or ball, clean the creases of your baby's legs and her upper thighs. Wipe downward, away from your child's body. If your child is a boy, use a fresh wipe to clean around his penis and testicles.

3 Take hold of your baby's ankles and lift up her bottom. If your child is a girl, clean around – but not inside – her vulva, using a fresh wipe for each pass. Always be careful to wipe from front to back, away from the vulva, to avoid transferring bacteria from the anus. Then clean the back of your baby's thighs and bottom. Gently pat dry.

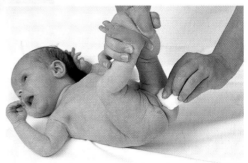

WATCH POINT...

Never attempt to clean under the foreskin of an uncircumcised boy – it is very tight during the first years of life, and pulling it back may cause damage. As your baby grows older, the foreskin will retract more easily. In the meantime it does not need cleaning.

Little boys often start peeing when their nappy is removed at changing time, so before removing it completely, hold the front of your child's nappy over his penis for a few seconds.

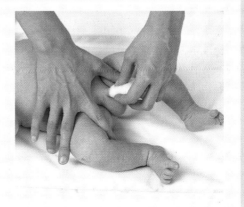

CLEANING A BOY

Putting on a new nappy

Once your baby's nappy area is clean and dry, it is a good idea to leave the nappy off for a while to give her bottom a chance air. If you wish, you can also apply a small amount of a specially formulated barrier cream to help protect her delicate skin against irritation.

Disposable nappies are fairly straightforward to put on, once you get the hang of them, and pre-shaped fabric nappies usually fit on in much the same way. Unshaped fabric nappies can be a little more tricky, not least because the fabric squares can be folded in different ways to suit the size of the baby and the absorbency required.

The kite fold (bottom right) is one of the most useful for growing babies because it is easy to adjust the size. The rectangle fold is even simpler to make – fold the fabric square in half to make a rectangle, then fold one of the shorter sides about a third of the way into the middle. This thicker area can be placed to the front for boys, and under the bottom for girls.

PUTTING ON A DISPOSABLE NAPPY

1 Take hold of your baby by his ankles, and gently lift up his bottom. Slide the opened nappy underneath his bottom, with the sticky tabs to the top. Bring the bottom of the nappy up between your baby's legs. Make sure that a baby boy's penis points downwards, to prevent him urinating into the waistband of the nappy.

2 Hold the front of the nappy firmly over your baby's tummy and stick down one side. Make sure that the nappy is not twisted and fits snugly around the thighs. There should be just enough room to fit one finger between the waist of the nappy and your baby's tummy. Stick down the other side. If it is too tight or too loose, unpeel the tabs and reposition.

PUTTING ON A FOLDED FABRIC NAPPY

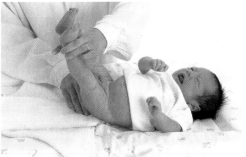

1 Fold the fabric square into your preferred nappy shape, unless the fabric is already pre-shaped, and lay it down on the changing mat or towel. Gently place your child onto the nappy. Take hold of your baby by her ankles and slide the nappy underneath her bottom so that the top side of the fabric aligns with her waist.

2 Take hold of the bottom of the nappy and bring the fabric up between your baby's legs, making sure a baby boy's penis is tucked downwards. Bring in the sides, pulling the nappy quite tight – it will loosen a little when you pin it.

3 Slide your fingers between the nappy and your baby's skin so you don't prick her, and carefully pin the sides. Adjust the fit so it fits snugly – it should be just loose enough to slip a finger down the side. If you like, you can put a pair of plastic pants over the top.

THE KITE FOLD

1 Lay the fabric nappy square down on a flat surface and bring two adjoining sides into the centre to produce a kite shape.

2 Fold the two points of the kite into the centre, and adjust the point at which they meet to alter the size. Align the longer top edge with your baby's waist and bring the shorter edge between her legs.

nappy rash

Your baby's skin is almost half the thickness of an adult's and very delicate, which is why you are unlikely to get through the nappy years without experiencing nappy rash at least once.

Nappy rash usually occurs when your baby's urine reacts with his faeces, causing a bacterial conversion of the urine to ammonia. This creates an alkaline that irritates his skin. Another factor can be the nappy itself rubbing on your child's skin as he moves, while perfumes, detergents and some of the chemicals used in nappies, wipes and lotions may also irritate sensitive skin. Nappy rash is most common in three- to six-month-old babies, although it is less common in breast-fed babies as breast milk makes their urine more acidic, countering the effect of the ammonia.

Allow your baby to spend some time each day without a nappy on. Letting light and air get to his bottom will help speed the healing process.

BARTY'S RASH

I changed from cloth nappies to disposables when Barty was three months old. At first I thought they were wonderful because they seemed to remain dry for ages. Then Barty developed nappy rash. His little bottom was bright red and he was obviously uncomfortable. When I thought about it, I realized that because the disposables were more absorbent and Barty hadn't obviously been wet, I had been leaving the nappies on for ages. Once I started changing them more frequently his nappy rash soon disappeared.

Recognizing the signs

The rash can vary from mild redness through to painful sores, and usually affects the buttocks, genitals and inner thighs. It can be particularly bad in the folds and creases of your baby's skin. The affected area often has spots around the edge.

Nappy rash can sometimes be aggravated by infection from a yeast-like organism commonly called thrush. Suspect infection if the rash persists, if the skin develops blisters or white patches, or if there is any pus. Always consult your doctor or other healthcare provider, who may recommend an anti-fungal cream suitable for treating candidal nappy rash.

Prevention

As with most things, prevention is better than a cure. Try to keep your baby's skin as dry and clean as possible and don't forget to change disposables regularly, even if they appear dry. Clean your baby's nappy area thoroughly at each nappy change, paying particular attention to the creases and folds. Gently pat his skin dry and use a barrier cream to protect the skin from contact with faeces and urine. Allow your baby time to kick without a nappy on each day. You could also try giving your child a little cranberry juice at bedtime, since this will help make his urine more acidic, discouraging the growth of bacteria.

TREATING NAPPY RASH

1 Change wet or soiled nappies quickly and regularly. Before removing the nappy, take hold of your baby's ankles and lift her bottom up into the air. This way the nappy will not rub against the irritated area as you slide it out from underneath her bottom.

2 Gently but thoroughly clean your child's nappy area (see p.25), patting the skin rather than rubbing to avoid further irritation. Use a mild baby wipe or cotton wool and water. Babies with very sensitive skin will do best with plain water.

3 Apply a specially formulated nappy rash cream to the affected area to help soothe and heal the skin. Spread the cream thinly so that it doesn't interfere with the absorbency of the nappy. Put the nappy on loosely, and snip a little of the elastic around the legs to let in air.

other possible problems

No matter how much care and attention you lavish on your baby's bottom, it is unlikely that the first few years of life will go by without a few problems. Your baby's delicate and still-developing digestive system is particularly susceptible to problems such as constipation or diarrhoea. If your baby does have difficulties, take comfort in the fact that he is not alone – very few babies are lucky enough to have completely trouble-free bottoms.

Urinary tract infections

It is important to take your child to see a doctor or other healthcare provider if you suspect that he has a urinary tract infection (UTI), since most will clear up quickly with antibiotics. Signs to look out for include any or all of the following: peeing more frequently than normal, fever, irritability, lack of interest in food, nausea and vomiting, general ill health, urine with an unusual smell and a tummy ache.

Treatment

You should encourage your child to drink plenty of water as this will help to cleanse the urinary tract of bacteria, but don't try to force your child to drink more than he needs. The doctor will usually prescribe antibiotics to treat the infection, and your child may show an improvement after taking two or three doses. Don't be tempted to stop the treatment before the course is finished, as infections can return if the drug is stopped too soon. Further investigations may need to be carried out to see if your child has scarred kidneys or an abnormality of the urinary tract.

Too much fruit juice can trigger diarrhoea, especially in young children. Juice is fine for older children, provided their intake is not excessive, but it should always be well diluted if diarrhoea is a problem.

Blood in urine

Urine that is red or tinged with red may indicate bleeding in the urinary tract and your child should see a doctor or other healthcare provider urgently. He will usually be given a urine test in order to identify the cause, and may need other diagnostic tests, too. If a kidney problem is suspected, your child may need to be treated in hospital. Bear in mind that drinking some dark-coloured liquids such as blackcurrant juice can cause alarming, but harmless, changes in the colour of your child's urine.

Diarrhoea

Mild diarrhoea is common in babies and young children and is usually due to germs, a new food or even too much fruit juice. Provided the diarrhoea clears up within a couple of days and your child is happy, urinating as frequently as usual and shows no other signs of illness (other than perhaps a slight loss of appetite), this is not usually anything to worry about. Give your child extra water, well-diluted fruit juice or an electrolyte replacement solution, and continue with his regular diet, including breast milk or formula for babies.

Severe diarrhoea

If your child has severe diarrhoea – when the loose stools last for more than a couple of days, or more than just a few extra stools are passed in a day – you should consult your doctor or your usual healthcare provider. Your child may need medical treatment as there is a risk of dehydration. If the diarrhoea is caused by an infection (watch for vomiting or fever) your doctor may prescribe antibiotics, although this will not help viral infections so your doctor may wish to take a stool sample first. Another possible explanation for the diarrhoea is that your child may be having difficulty digesting a

If you are worried your child may have urinary problems, a simple check for the presence of blood or bacteria in her urine can confirm whether there is an infection or any irritation of the urinary tract.

new food. The condition usually disappears once the offending food has been removed from his diet, and your doctor may decide to put your child on an elimination diet to try to identify the problem. Your child needs a healthy well-balanced diet, however, so never totally exclude a food without first consulting a doctor or dietitian. Keep your child well hydrated, and always consult your doctor before giving your child any medication for the diarrhoea.

Constipation

It is not the number of bowel movements that indicates constipation but the texture of the stools: your child is constipated if he has hard, dry stools that are difficult to pass. Constipation is often connected to what your child has been eating or drinking, and a lack of fibre or fluid can be responsible, although some children are also affected by upsets or changes in routine.

Bottle-fed babies may suffer from constipation if they are not getting enough at each feed, their feeds are incorrectly mixed or they are dehydrated. Once you start weaning your baby onto solids you may find that certain foods cause constipation. You will recognize the signs if your child has hard-to-pass stools the day after a certain food has been eaten. Severe constipation over a long period may be caused by a lack of thyroid hormone, or Hirschsprung's disease (see p.13), and will need medical investigation.

Treatment

Babies may be helped by increasing their fluid intake. Older children can benefit from extra fibre in their diet so include plenty of fruit, vegetables and cereals. If you suspect a particular

---

THE FIBRE CONTENT OF COMMON FOODS

Although children do not need a diet high in fibre, some fibre is necessary to ensure a healthy digestive system and to prevent constipation. For children over the age of two, the American Dietetic Association recommends using the formula 'your child's age plus 5' to calculate the minimum number of grams of fibre your child should be eating each day.

It is important that your child also drinks plenty of clear fluids – lack of fluids is a very common cause of constipation.

source	1	2	3	4	5	6	7	8	9	10*	source
Wholemeal flour											Cabbage
Wholemeal bread											Sweetcorn
White bread											Potatoes
Brown rice											Lima beans
White rice											Baked beans (canned)
Cornflakes											Peas
Apples											Apricots
Bananas											Prunes
Avocados											Dates
Carrots											Raisins
Spinach											Almonds

* Number of grams of fibre per 100 grams of each food

Severe constipation can be very painful and should always be treated by a doctor, so keep an eye on your child's toilet habits to check he is not suffering in silence.

food is responsible for your child's constipation, try eliminating it from his diet for a few days and then offer it again. If the result is the same, you will know to reduce the amount offered or to avoid that particular food for a few weeks before introducing it again. You are likely to find that a food that is a problem in the early stages of weaning ceases to be a problem as your child gets

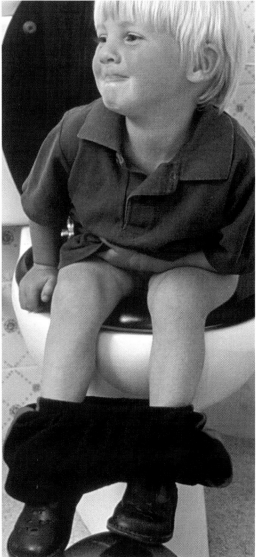

| 1 | 2 | 3 | 4 | 5 | 6 | 7 | 8 | 9 | 10* |

older. If your child has a longer-term intolerance to a certain food it may be necessary to avoid it altogether, but you should never totally exclude a food from your child's diet without first consulting a doctor or dietitian.

If the constipation becomes a problem your doctor may suggest stool softeners that make the stools easier to pass. Laxatives shouldn't be given to young children unless recommended by your doctor or healthcare provider.

Food allergy and intolerance

Persistent diarrhoea can be a sign of an allergy or intolerance to a particular food. This may be accompanied by a rash, changes in behaviour or sleeplessness. The word 'allergy' is often used to describe any abnormal reaction to a food, but a true allergic response must involve your child's immune system. It is relatively rare, and usually will result in some type of skin rash. Food intolerance is far more common, and simply describes a child's inability to digest, or oversensitivity to, a certain food – lactose in milk, for example, or gluten in wheat.

Treatment

Avoidance is the best way to deal with an allergy or intolerance, but it is not a good idea to permanently exclude a food from your child's diet without first seeking professional advice. Your doctor or dietitian will be able to help you ensure that your child has a well-balanced, healthy diet. Breast-feeding can help keep your child from developing allergies, and it is also a good idea to introduce foods into your child's diet gradually. The most common childhood allergens are cows' milk, diary products, eggs, citrus fruits and wheat.

Bloody stools

Small streaks of blood on the outside of your child's stools may be caused by an anal fissure, a small crack in the delicate mucus membrane of the anus which bleeds when pressure is put on it by hard stools. This is not serious and usually will respond to home treatment. Try to keep your child's stools soft by including plenty of liquid and fibre in his diet, and ask your pharmacist about specially formulated creams to lubricate your child's anus and promote healing. If the problem continues, you should discuss your child's constipation with your doctor.

Large amounts of blood in the stools are rare but may occur as a result of severe diarrhoea, intussusception (where part of the intestine telescopes in on itself) or from a malformation of the intestines. Always seek medical advice immediately. The treatment your child is given will depend on the cause of the bleeding, and hospital treatment may be needed.

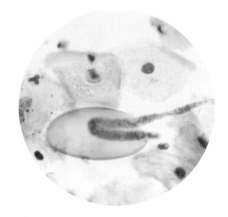

Pinworms live in the lower intestine and bowel of infected children. They come out of the anus at night to lay their eggs, and can be seen on the skin or in stools.

Pinworms

Also known as threadworms, because of their thread-like appearance, these tiny worms are usually harmless. They do, however, cause itching, and disturbed sleep. Your doctor will be able to give your child medication, usually in a single dose, which may need to be repeated a couple of weeks later. You may be advised to treat the whole family. You will need to make sure that your child's bedding and pyjamas are washed to remove any eggs, and you should keep your child's fingernails trimmed to prevent him damaging his skin as he scratches.

Bladder and bowel control

Although your baby's urinary and digestive systems are essentially the same as those of an adult, his immaturity in the early years means that his actions are automatic rather than controlled. As your child's nervous system develops, this automatic mechanism is gradually replaced by a voluntary one – an essential precursor to beginning successful potty training. But many other factors – from your child's social and psychological development, to your own attitudes and demands – are just as important when it comes to deciding exactly when to start your child's potty training.

your child's development

The age at which individual children are ready to leave behind their dirty nappies can vary enormously. In general girls tend to be ready for potty training a little earlier than boys, and become dry and clean more quickly. For both boys and girls, however, the age at which a child is ready to begin potty training will depend largely upon the rate of his or her own physical and emotional development.

Physical readiness

Before your child can begin to control when she has a bowel movement or passes urine, the sphincter muscles that control her bladder and bowel need to mature. Bladder control tends to be slower to develop than bowel control because it is easier for the anal sphincter to hold in solid matter than it is for the urethral sphincter to hold in urine. As the bladder matures, its ability to retain urine increases, so that by around 15 months many children can go for up to two hours without a wet nappy. You also may notice that your child wakes up dry after a nap. At around the same time you also may notice that your child has developed some natural bowel control and has fairly regular bowel movements with soft, formed stools.

Physical control

Your child also needs to be aware of the feelings associated with wetting or dirtying her nappy before she can learn to interpret these as a signal that she needs to pee or do a poop. Once she

Children develop the physical and emotional skills needed to use the potty at very different ages – but having brothers or sisters to copy can give a child a good head start when it comes to getting the hang of the basics.

Before your child is ready to use the potty, he has to develop the necessary physical coordination to be able to pull down his pants and sit on the potty.

begins to recognize these sensations she will naturally start to use the muscles associated with them, and as these become stronger her ability to control them will increase. Some babies' nervous systems mature enough to complete voluntary control of the sphincter muscles as early as a year, but this is the exception rather than the rule. Generally, children reach this stage of physical maturity sometime between the ages of 18 and 24 months, although some may be nearer 36 months before they are ready.

Physical coordination

Your child needs to be able to sit comfortably and securely on a potty or toilet seat, so coordination also plays a part in her physical readiness. She also should be able to manage her own clothing, as being able to pull her own underpants up and down is an integral part of potty training and gaining independence. Once potty training progresses to using the toilet, your child will need to be able to wipe herself, flush the toilet and wash her hands.

Signs of physical awareness

As your child's awareness grows, she may begin to indicate to you in signs or sounds that she is wet or dirty. Some children show awareness of the need to poop or of having passed a stool by stopping what they are doing for a few moments, or through their facial expression. Others are able to indicate with words that they are wet or dirty and may show signs of being unhappy until they have been cleaned up.

A growing interest in the contents of the nappy is also a sign of your child's increasing awareness and is quite normal. Some children become quite possessive about their poop and show a great deal of pride in it by wanting to smell and touch it. Seeing what her body has produced will help your child connect the feelings she had while having a bowel movement, with her poop. This will make the whole experience more real to her and help her to understand what is happening when she experiences these sensations.

CHILD'S PLAY

Learning through play

Your child can learn a lot through play, so encourage her to sit a teddy or doll on a potty or on the toilet and talk to her about what it is she is doing. If the toy falls into the toilet don't make a fuss, just remove it, give it a wash and allow your child to continue playing. This way your child will come to realize that if she falls into the toilet she will also be rescued and not flushed away.

Emotional readiness

Even if your toddler is physically mature enough for potty training, she may not yet be emotionally ready to give up wearing nappies, even if they are wet or dirty. After all, nappies are all your child has known since birth, so wearing them is normal for her, whereas sitting on a potty or the toilet is not. Your child may need time to come round to the idea, and reassurance that you are not going to make her use a potty or toilet until she is ready. Once she feels confident enough to give up her nappies she will be ready to begin potty training.

Coping with fears

Some children are scared of using the potty or toilet. Your child may dislike the idea of something that comes out of her – and which she may see as a part of her body – disappearing down the toilet. She even may be afraid that she could fall down the toilet and be flushed away.

If your child seems fearful or reluctant, don't force her to use the potty or toilet seat. You will only find yourself engaged in a battle of wills that

will be counter-productive to toilet training. Instead, you can encourage her to sit on her potty or toilet seat fully clothed a couple of times each day, perhaps after breakfast and before bed, so that she gets into a routine before you start training. You can make this into a special time by sitting with her and reading a story or chatting to her about the day's events. You could even give your child a toy that she's only allowed to play with when she's on the potty. Once she has got used to the idea that this potty time is a normal, everyday experience she will gradually learn to overcome her fears.

Avoiding conflict

Physical readiness often occurs at the same time as the stage often referred to as 'the terrible twos'. This is when your child challenges everything you want her to do. Although it is perfectly normal for a toddler who is learning to be independent to behave in this way, this is not a good time to try to introduce the potty. Wait until your child reaches a more cooperative phase when she is more likely to go along with your suggestions and be willing to cooperate with you. Once your child shows signs that she is interested in using the potty or toilet, she is emotionally ready for training.

Verbal readiness

Your child needs to be able to communicate with you her need to pee or poop, so some verbal ability is needed. She also needs to be able to understand simple instructions, even if her own language is very limited. She will need a toileting vocabulary that is understandable not only to people in your home, but also to outside caregivers, child care providers and other parents. Words that are only familiar to you and your immediate family won't help your child if she needs to go when she is with other people outside your home.

Social readiness

You may find it hard to imagine that there is a social side to using a potty or toilet, but your child will learn a lot through watching and imitating you and others. Encourage your child to come with you when you go to the bathroom so she can see how adults use the toilet, and let her do the flushing when you have finished. Put her potty in the bathroom, so that she can sit on it at the same time.

At first, just let her sit with her nappy on and don't expect any success. Use this as a time for her to become accustomed to the potty. Talk to her about what you are doing and explain to her that she'll be able to use the toilet one day too, just like a grown-up.

Pushing your child into using the potty before she feels ready, or when she is going through a negative phase can be counter-productive, making her resentful and unwilling to learn.

Copying others

Seeing another child near her age perform on the toilet will help make it seem a more achievable possibility for your toddler. If there are brothers, sisters or cousins around, your child will naturally want to copy what they do and can learn a lot from their example. In the same way, if your child is in nappies when she starts at nursery or in childcare you may find that a previously unmotivated child suddenly shows a lot more interest in using the potty. Wanting to be like her peers is often all the encouragement your child needs.

CHECK LIST

You will know whether your child is ready to begin potty training when he:

☑ Wants to come to the bathroom with you and understands what the toilet is for.

☑ Knows what it means to have a wet or dirty nappy and perhaps shows a preference for being clean and dry.

☑ Seems to recognize at least a few seconds ahead that he needs to go.

☑ Says words that seem to indicate he wants to pee or poop.

☑ Stays dry for an hour-and-a-half to two hours at a time.

☑ Shows a desire for independence by wanting to do things for himself.

☑ Does not show concern about sitting on the potty or toilet.

☑ Is over the fascination of learning to walk and run and enjoys sitting still and playing with his toys.

☑ Is in a willing, receptive mood rather than in a negative phase.

☑ Shows a desire to wear big kid's underpants and attempts to pull them up and down without help.

☑ Has regular bowel movements.

☑ Can follow simple directions, such as those for washing his hands.

The right time for you

It is almost as important for you to be ready to potty train as it is for your child to be ready for potty training. You will need to be calm and relaxed about the whole process and be prepared for it to take time. If you become anxious, frustrated or angry when your child has an accident or the floor gets wet or dirty from spills, she will start to associate these negative feelings with the potty.

Times to avoid

If at all possible, you should avoid starting potty training during a busy time in your life, such as at Christmas, when you are about to move to a new house or a when a new baby is due to arrive. Your child is going to need a lot of attention, especially when you first start, and trying to potty train her when there are a lot of other things going on will only make you both stressed. Very young children unconsciously pick up and reflect their parent's feelings, and if you are stressed your child is likely to feel it, too. This then becomes a no-win situation and may well turn into a battle of wills, which certainly won't make potty training any easier.

On the other hand, you can't keep holding off forever, so if there is no clear break for you in sight and your child is raring to go, you may decide it is best to get started anyway.

attitudes towards starting potty training

In the past there was a view that the earlier you could train your baby the more successful you were as a parent. Today's attitude to potty training is very different, and becoming clean and dry is seen as the child's achievement rather than the parent's. Many experts believe the emphasis should be on potty 'learning' – something the child does – rather than potty 'training' – something the parent does.

Of course, it is easy to feel that you have 'failed' if your child is still in nappies after the age of three, but you should remember that your child is in control of his body, not you, and he will become potty trained when he is ready.

Common concerns

You will probably find that anyone who has ever potty trained a child has advice and opinions to offer you. Grandmothers are likely to tell you that they started early and achieved success at an age when today's parents haven't even begun. This was probably possible because more mothers were at home and had time to dedicate to potty training. Add to this the fact that babies wore cloth nappies and there were not the same washing and drying facilities available, and you can see why early training was attractive. This does not mean very early training is always the best option for modern parents.

Different generations often have different attitudes towards potty training, but there are no right or wrong answers – you'll need to decide what works best for you.

Some parents believe in starting training while their child is very young, but this can take much more time and effort to be successful.

Different approaches

There are many different views on the best way to go about getting your child out of nappies, but in the end it comes down to finding or adapting a method that best suits you, your baby and your personal circumstances. Although there are no hard and fast rules, you may like to consider the following four basic approaches to achieving potty-training success.

Very early training

Some parents still believe that it is never too early to start potty training, and start holding their baby on the potty when they are only a few months old. This approach does have some success as it is possible to 'catch' a pee or poop in a potty if your baby goes regularly, such as after a feed. By sitting your baby on a potty at the same time each day you condition his nervous system so that he will begin to perform automatically when he feels the potty under him.

There also used to be a belief that a child who achieved early training was more intelligent. This theory has since been disproved and we now know that there is very little connection between early toilet training and IQ. Another belief, which some parents still have, is that 'doing it wrong' could cause deep psychological scars. Learning to control his bodily functions is a natural step in your child's development, and providing he is physically and emotionally ready and learns through gentle encouragement rather than anger and punishment, there is no reason why he should feel anything other than growing independence once it is achieved.

TRAINING SARA

I took my mum's advice and started sitting Sara on the potty when she was a few months old. By 14 months she was able to tell me when she wanted to poop, but getting her dry took much longer. I was putting her on the potty seven or eight times a day until she was two-and-a-half and she wasn't fully trained until her third birthday. Some of my friends didn't start training until their kids were over two and achieved success in a couple of months. It took me over two years!

Some parents prefer to wait until their child shows a definite interest in using the potty before beginning training, so that he'll be more cooperative and enthusiastic.

Although this will save you a dirty or wet nappy, it is important to realize that your baby isn't voluntarily controlling his actions. In fact, some experts believe that introducing the potty this early can cause a child to rebel later when he starts being able to control the reflexes himself, which can make the whole potty-training process much more prolonged.

Child-led training

As your child gets older, usually sometime between his second and third birthday, he becomes capable of deciding for himself when he wants to give up wearing nappies and start using the potty or toilet. Once he has reached this stage, taking him out of nappies generally results in only a short period of accidents before he is both clean and dry.

Although it means a longer period in nappies, child-led training removes many of the stresses associated with potty training as there is no conflict of interests between you and your child. If you decide on this approach you will find it works best if your child has an awareness of the contents of his nappies and some understanding of what a potty or toilet is used for.

Adult-led training

If you can't wait for your child to decide for himself that he wants to be potty trained, perhaps because a place at a nursery is dependent on him being out of nappies, you can decide for yourself when to start. Providing your child is physically and emotionally ready, with a little encouragement he will gradually learn what you expect of him. The length of time this may take varies from child to child. Some get the hang of it in a few weeks, others take several months. Occasionally it just doesn't work and if this is the case it is best to revert to nappies for the time being and try again when the child is older and more able to cooperate.

Intensive training

This method can be very successful with an older toddler who has perhaps rejected the idea of potty training at an earlier age. Of course, there is no reason why you shouldn't try it as your first option, providing your child is ready and you are able to commit time solely to potty training, without any interruptions. The idea is to create a situation in which your child is able to recognize and respond to the need to pee within a very

Giving your child lots of drinks, so that he needs to pee more often, can help him get the hang of using the potty more quickly.

DAVID'S POTTY DAY

It was summer and David was two-and-a-half when I decided that we would give up nappies. I had read about intensive training, and it seemed a better idea than weeks or months of accidents and mess. We spent the day in the garden so that he didn't have to wear a nappy and it didn't matter if he had an accident. We did a lot of potty talk, with plenty of praise and encouragement when he did something in the potty. I gave him extra drinks so that he needed to pee frequently, which helped too.

By the end of the first day he knew what was expected of him and by the second day he was going to the potty without being reminded. He even managed to pull his trainer pants up and down himself. He was dry at night at the same time, so for us intensive training worked really well.

short time. This requires dedication on your part – you'll need to give him a few days of undivided attention – but it can be a good way to get everything out of the way at once.

You'll need to give your child plenty of drinks, encourage him to use the potty on his own, and give him lots of rewards for dry underpants. Try to make the whole thing like a fun game, but don't let him get overexcited – remain firm but encouraging throughout. Once he has got the hang of peeing in the potty, learning to poop should soon follow.

4 Getting ready for potty training

Once you feel that your toddler is physically and emotionally ready to begin, you will need to start laying the groundwork. Get your child involved from the very start by taking her out with you to buy a new potty – there are all sorts of fun and exciting types for you both to choose from – and consider investing in some attractive new training pants so she will really feel motivated to keep herself dry. Get your little novice feeling really comfortable and familiar with her new potty, so that it holds no fears for her when you start training in earnest. A little preparation goes a long way when when it comes to getting your child clean, dry and happy.

choosing the right time to start

Once you think your child is physically and emotionally ready to begin potty training, you will need to choose the best time to start, and decide on a plan of action. A lot will depend on whether you are happy to allow your child to take the initiative, or if you want to move things along yourself. Either way, finding the right time will save you a great deal of trouble and effort.

Is there a right time of year?

If you live in an area with hot summers and cool winters, you'll find that the warmer months are definitely the best time to start potty training.

Your child will be wearing light, easy to manage clothes, such as shorts or summer dresses, which removes the need for her to manage woolly tights or thick, often cumbersome trousers. If your child only has to manage pulling her underpants down and then up again she will find it a lot easier to get to the potty in time to perform. And if there are accidents, you won't have so many layers to wash.

If the weather is warm enough, you can start training outside in the garden. This will make it much easier to clean up after any accidents, and your child will love spending a few days running around in the open air.

If the weather is really warm, wearing no clothes at all will make it much simpler for your child to get to the potty in time.

Times to avoid

Even if your child is showing all the signs of readiness, there are times when it may be better to delay potty training for a short while. If any of the following apply, then you probably will be better off waiting a bit longer:

✔ You and your partner are having problems, or there is some other form of conflict within the family that is causing upset and emotionally affecting your child. Don't start potty training until things have settled down.

✔ You have just moved your child into a big bed, or you have only recently stopped breast feeding – he will probably need a few weeks to adjust to this change before you introduce another.

✔ You have just moved house. Your child is likely to be feeling insecure about his new surroundings, so give him time to get used to his new environment.

✔ You have just returned to work, or your child's usual caregiver has changed. A change in caregiver often upsets a child, so this may not be the best time to start.

✔ Your child is going through a negative phase. There is no point trying to teach your child to use the potty if he is not in a receptive frame of mind. If his favourite word is 'no', and he doesn't want to do anything to please you, wait until he has reached a more positive phase before introducing the potty.

✔ You are just about to have, or have just had a new baby. Your toddler may be feeling rather insecure and anxious about his position in the family, so it would be better to wait until he has adapted to the changes.

Winter warmers

Of course, it is perfectly possible to potty train your child during colder weather. Domestic heating usually means that the home is warm and snug throughout the colder months, although you may want to turn the thermostat up in the room where your child is going to use the potty so that it's more cozy. Your child is less likely to want to bare her bottom if it means getting cold.

If possible, place the potty on top of a plastic sheet or on a floor that is easy to clean. That way, any accidents can be mopped up with the minimum of fuss. Cleaning pee and poop off a thick-pile carpet is no fun at all.

Clearing your schedule

Your child's first introduction to serious potty training needs to be carried out during a period when you can give her a lot of extra attention. Even if you have only a weekend to spare, this should be long enough to get her to understand the principles of what you want her to do – provided she has your undivided attention.

It may take weeks, or even months, for your child to completely master all the techniques, but it is these early days that lay the foundation for eventual success, so allow enough time to do things thoroughly.

You'll need plenty of time during the early stages of potty training so that you can give your child all of the attention she needs.

HOLLY'S NEW HOUSE

We were moving house and I thought it would be a good idea to get Holly, who was 20 months old, potty trained before the move. She got the hang of it very quickly and was dry during the day within a week. But once we moved, she started wetting herself again. I was at my wit's end trying to cope with the unpacking, changing Holly four or five times a day and doing all the extra washing and ironing. There simply weren't enough hours in the day! It took weeks to get her dry again. The move obviously upset her and I wish now I'd waited until we'd settled in to our new home before trying to potty train her.

Many parents find that holidays are a good time to start. The pace of life is less frantic and you will be more relaxed and able to give your child your undivided attention. Also, your partner may be around to share in the training, showing your child that both mum and dad are interested in her ability to use the potty.

Holidays away from home can also be a good time to start – if your toddler is running about bare-bottomed on the beach you'll certainly have less cleaning up to do. Bear in mind, however, that your child will have lots of other distractions, and that she may relapse once back in familiar surroundings. Changes in diet while on holiday can change your child's bowel habits, which can also affect toilet-training success.

buying a potty

A month or two before you start training you will need to buy a potty, or more than one if you want to have one both upstairs and downstairs. This way your child can become accustomed to having a potty around before any serious training takes place. Before you go shopping for your potty explain to your child what you are going to buy and in simple terms what it is used for, and take him with you to the shops so he can help you choose one he likes. Also, get your child to try prospective potties out for size first, so that you can make sure he's comfortable on it.

Picking the perfect potty

Potties are usually made from plastic and are available in many different shapes, styles and colours. They vary in price as much as they do in style, with some of the most expensive ones designed to look like miniature toilets. Others play music or make a noise, and there are even potties that come complete with a tray for drinks and toys. See the chart on p.50 for a comparison of the advantages and disadvantages of some of the most common types of potty.

Splashguards

Most potties have a splashguard incorporated into their shape, others come with detachable splashguards or deflectors. Boys should be taught to sit with these at the front, while girls should sit with these at the back. Childcare experts have expressed concern that little boys can hurt themselves on the detachable splashguard and the experience may make them reluctant to use the potty again, so if you go for this type it may be wise to remove the deflector before use.

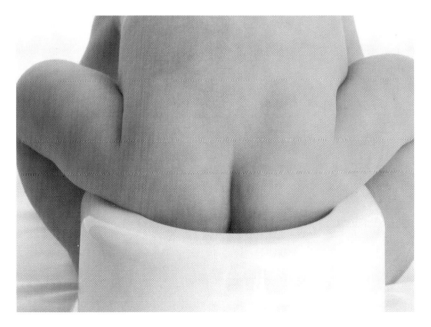

Before you begin toilet training you'll need to choose a potty that will fit your baby's little bottom snugly although not too snugly – and that he can call his own.

CHOOSING YOUR POTTY

Potties come in all shapes and sizes, and vary in price as much as they do in style. Whichever type of potty you decide on, the most important factor is that it sits solidly on the floor without tipping or sliding, has no sharp edges, can be emptied quickly and is easy to clean.

	Advantages	Disadvantages
	Regular-shaped potties are cheap, simple and effective, and are easy to pick up and empty. Their function is clear cut from the start.	The potty may not seem fun or diverting enough to appeal to your child – if your child isn't interested in his potty, you might have trouble motivating him to use it.
	Potties which are chair-shaped or designed to look like miniature toilets are perfect for a child who wants to copy his parents. When your child gets older, it may be easier for him to make the transition to a proper toilet.	This type of potty is sometimes more expensive, and can be awkward to use – it encourages a sitting rather than squatting position, which can actually make it more difficult to push when doing a poop.
	Potties that play music or make a noise when your child pees or poops into them help your toddler realize when he produces something, and are great for stimulating his interest.	Your child will quickly realize that he can make the noise play by dropping toys or other objects into the potty. This fascination with the music or sound effects may well outlast your own patience.
	Potties shaped like animals or cars are easily incorporated into everyday play, and your child may be more keen to use a potty that looks fun or exciting.	There is a danger that your child may want to play with the potty when it is full, or pee and poop in it when there are toys inside. You need to consider whether you want the potty to be used as a play item, or whether its function should be distinct.

Buying a special toilet seat

Rather than starting with a potty, you – or your child – may prefer the idea of going straight into using the toilet. There is a drawback to this, because most children find doing a poop easier if they have their feet on the floor. It is more difficult to push if the feet are dangling. But if you think your child is capable of using the big toilet then it may be worth buying a child's seat.

Children often feel uncomfortable perched on an adult seat, and being tense isn't conducive to happy potty training. Your child can easily be frightened if he accidentally falls into the bowl and he may even hurt himself. A special child's seat will fit onto the adult toilet seat, making it smaller and more comfortable for little bottoms.

As your child will probably find it difficult to fit the seat on the toilet himself, it's a good idea to keep it in place all the time. Older children and adults can remove it when they need to use the toilet and then replace it. Your child will also need a small, sturdy stepping stool to help him climb on to the seat. This will also be useful when it comes to washing his hands as it will allow him to reach the tap handles unaided.

Travel potties

Some potties have lids, which have the advantage of keeping the contents secure and odours trapped until they can be emptied. This is particularly helpful on car journeys when the full potty can be stored in the boot until you can get rid of the contents. An alternative, when travelling, is a potty that folds flat for easy storage. It takes a disposable liner, which can be tied up after use, in the same way as a nappy-disposal bag.

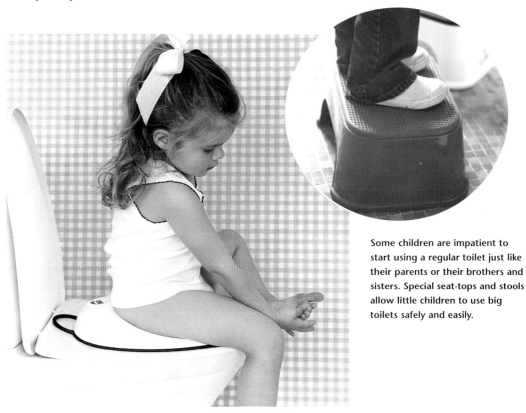

Some children are impatient to start using a regular toilet just like their parents or their brothers and sisters. Special seat-tops and stools allow little children to use big toilets safely and easily.

Help familiarize your child with his new potty by encouraging him to sit on it fully dressed and incorporate it into his play.

Introducing the potty

It is important for your child to understand the potty belongs to him and nobody else – allow your child to play with his potty and involve it in his daily routine so that he becomes used to it.

At first your child will probably only want to play with the potty, maybe putting toys in it or sitting a doll or teddy on it. Don't discourage this – once he is familiar with the potty he will be more likely to want to sit on it himself. Help encourage your child's potty-bonding by letting him personalize it with stickers, or write his name for him on the side of the potty.

Practising potty sitting

The next step is to encourage him to come with you to the bathroom and sit on the potty, fully clothed, while you are using the toilet. This allows him to get used to the feel of sitting on the potty without having to bare his bottom. Don't force your child to sit on the potty unless he wants to and don't suggest that he actually use it unless he expresses a desire to do so. After all, your toddler is used to wearing a nappy, which is reassuring and warm. For him, sitting on a potty is cold and strange in comparison.

Once your child is happy to sit on his potty, suggest that he tries it without a nappy. If you can, choose a time when your child is likely to do a poop so that he can see for himself what the potty is for. Don't worry if he doesn't do anything, your aim is to get him used to the feel of it against his bare skin. Make sure that the room you have the potty in is warm and cozy.

Creating a routine

Once your child is happy sitting on the potty without a nappy, you can start introducing a regular routine. Sit him on the potty before you dress him in the morning, and maybe again before bath time. Don't expect any success initially, just get him used to the idea that this is something that happens everyday.

Staying positive

If your child only wants to sit on the potty when he feels like it, or refuses to do so at all, be firm and tell him that this is what you want him to do. Explain that one day he will be able to do this by himself, just like a grown-up. Even if you can only get him to sit there for a few seconds, give him plenty of praise and encouragement. With practise, your child will come to accept this as part of his routine – an important step in the early stages of potty training.

moving on to underpants

Once your child shows signs of readiness and has had plenty of potty practice, try taking her out of nappies and putting her into disposable training pants, cloth training pants or underwear. This is one of the most effective techniques for rapid potty-training progress – wearing 'big kid's' underwear will make your child feel more mature and help her to understand that potty training is part of this new feeling.

Training pants

Like nappies, training pants are available in disposable or reusable cloth styles. They absorb pee and poop in much the same way as a nappy, but can be pulled up and down easily and look like normal underwear. The idea is that they are worn instead of nappies while your child is being trained, so that if an accident happens it is contained in the pants and doesn't come through

Dressing your child in training pants will make him feel more grown up and let him know that it's time to ditch the nappies.

EMMA'S NEW PANTIES

Training pants were a real help while I was potty training Emma. I used disposable ones with a cute design on them that faded when they became wet, so that Emma could see for herself when she'd had an accident. This made her very keen to stay dry and she was into proper panties in a matter of weeks.

the clothing. It's possible to get different absorbencies and thicknesses, so you can dress frequent wetters in nappy-like training pants, and progress to more lightweight versions.

Although they are a convenient way to bridge the gap between nappies and regular underwear, the drawback is that they are too much like a nappy. While wearing them your child won't have the same sensation of wetting or dirtying herself as she will wearing normal underwear. Despite this, many parents find them useful at the beginning of potty training, especially if a child is having frequent accidents.

Proper underwear

Don't put your child into proper underwear before she is ready – you'll only confuse her and give yourself more work. Wait until she shows signs of readiness and has had plenty of potty practise. Your child may even decide for herself that she doesn't want to wear nappies anymore. If this happens, seize the opportunity and take her out as soon as you can to buy her first panties or underpants.

Making your choice

Buy around half a dozen pairs to begin with, to make sure that you have enough to give her a clean pair when she has an accident, and go for cotton, which will be more absorbent than synthetic materials. Be sure to buy them big enough, so that she will be able to pull them up and down easily. Let her choose the ones she likes and reinforce her decision by telling her how grown up you think she is.

Fun and brightly-coloured underwear will inspire your child and make her feel grown up. They're not great at absorbing accidents though, so save them until your toddler's mastered all the basics!

Hyping it all up

If your child seems as though she is quite content to carry on wearing nappies forever, you may need to take the initiative yourself. Suggest to your child that you think it is time for her to start wearing proper underwear like a big girl. Let her get used to the idea and then, a few days later, tell her that you will be going shopping to buy some for her. Build your day out into a big adventure, and when the special day arrives, let her pick underwear she'll really want to wear.

When you get home, help your child remove her nappy and try on her new panties or underpants. Let her admire herself in the mirror and tell her what a big girl she is. Store her underwear in a drawer that she can reach so that she can get them herself when she is getting dressed in the morning.

other things to think about

Before you start potty training, there are a few other considerations to take into account. After all, it is no use teaching your child to use a potty if he is unable to make anyone outside your family understand when he needs to go, or if you have a caregiver who doesn't realize how best to back your efforts up. When it comes to potty training, preparation is everything.

Caregivers

If your toddler is in a nursery or childcare when you decide to start training you will need to enlist the help of his caregiver before you begin. You both need to be in agreement about how the training is to be done, so it is important to find out your caregiver's views. If you have a different approach you will need to discuss these differences. Don't do this while your child is listening as he will quickly sense that you are discussing something to do with him, which may lead to feelings of insecurity.

Successes and setbacks

Once potty training has started you should talk to his caregiver each day about his progress. It may be that your child is a little perturbed by the differences in surroundings or approach. On the other hand, you may find that your child shows more interest in using the potty at the childcare centre than he does at home because he sees all the other children using the potty or toilet, too.

A childcare centre can be a great place for your child to watch other kids using the potty, which will help her learn by example.

If this is the case, you need to take the lead from the caregiver and follow the routine he is used to at the centre when you are at home. Accidents are bound to happen, so always make sure your child has plenty of clean underwear and clothes for the caregiver to change him into.

Toilet talk

While you were changing your baby's nappy when he was younger, you probably used to chat to him about his bladder or bowel movements. If so, you probably have already formed some kind of language to describe these functions. The words you use will depend on what you and your family find acceptable. Most commonly used are words such as 'pee' and 'poop', though some people still prefer 'number one' for urine and

Most children have a fascination with their bodily products and sometimes talk about them loudly and at the most inappropriate times!

'number two' for a stool. Many parents still feel embarrassed about discussing intimate parts of the body and find it easier to use nicknames for the penis or the vagina. Whatever your feelings or qualms may be, there is nothing wrong about calling these parts by their correct names.

Sometimes names develop from a child's mispronunciation and get passed down the generations. Do remember, though, that cute or quirky names, which only your immediate circle of family and friends understand, won't be much use to your child when you are not around to translate. Your child is likely to use the words you choose frequently and often very loudly, so it's best to go for something that is generally recognized and acceptable outside of the home.

A word about diet

Although your child doesn't require any kind of special diet to achieve successful potty training, there are a few things you may want to consider. Both constipation and diarrhoea can cause difficulties and setbacks when you are potty training, so if your child has a natural tendency toward constipation, it is important to give him a diet that has plenty of fibre in it. Try to include daily portions of fruit and vegetables, and some wholemeal bread and pasta. Milk products and cooked carrots contribute to constipation, so try to limit these. You should also make sure that your toddler gets plenty of fluids.

Toddler diarrhoea, a persistent form of diarrhoea, may be caused by too many snacks or cold drinks on top of large meals. Keeping your child to three meals a day, with the occasional snack of fruit or raw vegetables such as carrot sticks, may help to relieve the condition.

Steps in training

Now that you're ready to begin helping your little one make the transition from nappies, it's time to start developing a potty routine. With a little bit of time and effort, you'll soon find your toddler gets the hang of the basics. The most important thing, once you start, is to remain calm, confident and consistent in your approach – there is no place for anger or punishment in potty training. Have fun, and you'll find that this time will be a rewarding and bonding experience for you both.

the potty-training routine

Now that you and your child are ready to start potty training, you will need to decide how you are going to go about it. Some parents find that a regular daily routine works best, others believe that taking a more casual approach is less stressful for both parent and child.

What you decide will depend a lot on your child's personality and may be influenced by your own toilet habits. If your toddler has a calm, compliant personality and her bowel movements are already fairly regular – perhaps she always passes a movement after breakfast – then a daily routine may work easily. If your child is particularly strong-willed or excitable, or there is no regular pattern to her bowel movements, trying to impose a daily routine may lead to confrontation and frustration.

Setting time aside

Start by sitting your child on the potty once or twice a day. Traditional advice suggests that after breakfast is the best time, but be flexible – if your child usually has a bowel movement at suppertime, there is little point in making her sit on the potty first thing in the morning. While

Try to get your child into a routine of sitting on the potty at around the same time each day, but never force him to stay on the potty if he wants to get off.

she is sitting, give her a biscuit, read to her or let her play with a special toy that she has only when she's using the potty. Don't make her stay sitting there for longer than five or ten minutes and never try to restrain her. Let her get up if she wants to, and don't scold her for not sitting for the appropriate length of time. You don't want your child to associate this time with stressful or negative feelings.

It goes without saying that your child should never be punished verbally or with a smack if she refuses to sit on the potty or won't perform in it. You can't force a child to do a bowel movement when you want her to; she has to learn to associate all the emotions and physical sensations of peeing and pooping with using the potty.

Taking the casual approach

If your toddler doesn't have regular bowel movements, sitting her on the potty at a certain time each day is likely to be pointless. It may be easier for you both if you watch for signs that she needs to go, and then suggest to her that it's time for her to use the bathroom. Once you have had some success, you can introduce the idea that she should tell you when she feels the need to pee or poop. Of course, she won't always remember, so you will still need to watch out for the tell-tale signs.

Accepting setbacks

Even if your child happily settles into a daily routine, be prepared for her to suddenly go off the idea. It may be that her bowel habits have changed, she may simply have become bored with the whole thing or she may see refusal to go as a means of getting your attention. In any case, you need to be careful not to make an issue of it, even though you may feel frustrated and annoyed. The best course of action is to drop the routine for a day or two, or even longer if your

You may be able to spot when your child needs to use the potty. Watch for signs such as clutching herself, swaying from side to side or squeezing her legs together.

child remains resistant. It is important not to turn potty training into a battle of wills between you and your child or to create an aversion to the routine that you are trying to impose.

Family toilet habits

Your approach may be influenced by your own bathroom habits. If you are used to having regular bowel movements at a certain time each day, you are more likely to favor a regular routine for your child. If you don't pay much attention to these bodily functions and just go when you feel the need, the casual approach is a more likely choice to take.

Your child may also be influenced by your attitude to the toilet. Some people spend the minimum time possible in the bathroom, others take a more leisurely approach, arming themselves with reading material and taking some time on the toilet. Children like to have role models, and if your child sees you spending time in the bathroom armed with a good book it would be unreasonable to expect her to perform to order with no distractions. Your child is more likely to perform if she is relaxed, so even if you do not spend any more time than is necessary in the bathroom, your child may benefit from having a book to read or a favourite toy to play with.

Creating the right atmosphere

The most important thing is for your child to find using the potty or toilet a peaceful experience, not rushed and tense. She needs to learn that her need to pee or poop is a perfectly routine occurence, and is just as important as eating, playing and having fun.

Praise and attention

It is easy to make potty training a family activity, with everyone giving praise and encouragement when your child uses the potty. This can be taken further, with grandparents, aunts and uncles being asked to admire the contents. Some children respond well to all this attention. For them, praise from admiring siblings and adults gives a sense of achievement.

Although such encouragement is an important part of potty training, it should not be so over the top that your child is made to feel that using the potty is a performance rather than a natural learning process. Teaching your child to use the potty may seem like the most important thing in your life at the time, but learning to be clean and dry is just another step towards independence and should be treated as such. Your child needs positive attention focused on all her achievements

Some children love to perform for their parents, relatives and siblings, and thrive on everyone's praise. Other children may be embarrassed by too much attention.

Dressing for success

Your toddler needs to be able to negotiate pulling her underwear down and up again by herself. Dressing your toddler in all-in-one suits, tights, or jeans with a zipper or belt will make this very difficult. At first, you may find it best to dress your child in loose clothing, such as tracksuit bottoms or a dress, and leave off any underwear. This makes it easy for her to manage her clothes. If your child is in training pants, using these with just a T-shirt will make life simple for her when she is at home.

and in these terms potty training should be treated no differently to her taking her first step, or saying her first words.

Privacy

Not all children enjoy being the centre of attention, and your child may be embarrassed by too much fuss. You know your child best – if she's shy and upset by too much attention, she may be happier for potty training to remain something that you do together privately, away from the rest of the family.

Some children start off being happy about the attention their success brings them and then, without any warning, develop a thing about privacy. Your toddler may hide in her bedroom every time she changes her underwear and may be offended if anyone tries to watch or help her. Try to respect these new feelings; this newfound modesty is a sign of her growing independence and self-awareness. She certainly won't want anyone with her in the bathroom if she's going through this phase.

Appropriate behaviour

All children have a right to privacy, and this needs to be respected. After all, your child will have to learn that although it is all right to be proud of her private parts, and nakedness is fine at home, it is not acceptable to go out without clothes or to touch her genitals in public.

There are, of course, occasions where it may not be possible to allow her complete privacy while using the toilet. Childcare centres, for example, don't usually allow total privacy in the bathroom. The same applies to public toilets, where a child will always need to be chaperoned. You need to explain to your child that different situations may require different behaviour. Once she understands, she will be starting to learn about boundaries and acceptable social behaviour.

Rewarding success

The most effective way to reward your child, while she's learning to use the potty, is with plenty of praise and loving attention. But you may find that offering your child a more tangible reward – such as a sweet or a biscuit – can also have some success and will help to reinforce the praise you give her. Your child may respond positively to such incentives because they give her a choice – she is not using the potty to please her parents, she is using it to get a treat. By letting your child have this choice you are giving her a feeling of independence and control, which may encourage her success.

If you do wish to use this type of incentive, try to remember that any reward you give needs to be immediate, with your child receiving her prize as soon as she performs. Suggesting that your child must stay dry for a day or a week before receiving a reward simply won't work, as time has very little meaning to a toddler.

Stars, stickers and reward charts

If you feel that a bigger treat, such as a toy, will be more effective, you may like to use a star chart to underline the connection between potty and reward. You can't give your child a toy every time she pees or poops in her potty, but you could introduce a system so that she earns a star each time she goes. These stickers can be placed on a chart and once she has earned enough stickers – this is something you need to make clear before you introduce the scheme – she will get her toy. For example, ten stickers could equal one toy. It is important to remember that this is a reward scheme and you should not remove stickers if your child has an accident – the idea is to reinforce her achievement, not draw attention to failure.

Even if you decide not to offer your child any other type of incentive, a bright, colourful star chart is still a great way to motivate a toddler. You can get your toddler really involved in the scheme by making the chart together and encouraging her to put on the stars or stickers herself. Even with no reward, sticking on stars for staying dry or using the potty successfully will give your child a real sense of achievement, and it is an excellent way to emphasize the praise that you give her.

Rather than encouraging your child to demand sweets or biscuits in exchange for using the potty, try offering a less tangible treat such as a fun day out, instead.

I thought that offering a reward for every success would quickly make Paul realize the advantages of going to the bathroom. It worked well at first and Paul would proudly show me what he'd done and get given a few jelly beans in return. Then he realized that not performing also gave him power over me. If he demanded something and I said 'no' he would promptly pee all over the floor.

have found the policy backfired because their child refused to use the potty unless she received a prize, even though she was able to control her bladder and bowels.

Keeping it simple

For any scheme to work, you will need to be clear about your aims and explain them in language your child can understand. It is also important to offer your child something that she really wants – if you offer a trip to the park when she really wants some sweets, you may be simply wasting your time.

Less tangible rewards

Many parents worry that offering a material reward is too much like bribery and gives the child the wrong message. You may feel that the offer of a less tangible incentive, such as a trip to the zoo or the park, is a good compromise between motivating your child and bribing her.

Your child, however, may find it difficult to see the connection between using her potty and receiving this kind of reward – after all, you won't be able to give her a day out every time she performs. For this reason, you may need to use some sort of star chart to make the link between using the potty and receiving a treat more obvious to your child.

Possible problems

Whatever type of incentive system you decide to use, it is important that your child does not learn to use the scheme to manipulate you. Some parents who have tried using reward schemes

Some children like fun, simple charts and are happy simply sticking on the stars. Others prefer more complex charts laid out week-by-week so they can see their progress over time. Whichever type you go for, make sure it's bright and full of colour.

potty training boys

As well as generally being slower than girls to become toilet trained, boys are often messier, so you can expect to clean up a lot of urine from the toilet floor. In the early months, it is a good idea to keep plenty of newspapers or paper towels in the bathroom to mop up any spills.

Boys are also more likely to play with their poop, and if this should happen, the best approach is to avoid showing disgust and to simply clean your son's hands as if they'd become muddy.

Standing up or sitting down

Your child will quickly make it clear whether he wants to stand up at the toilet and pee just like dad, or if he prefers to sit on the potty or toilet seat. Generally, little boys sit down to urinate during early toilet training. As bowel movements and urine often arrive at the same time, it makes sense for boys to sit down initially – at least until they can distinguish between what they have to do. Some boys prefer to sit facing the back of the toilet to begin with, before moving on to standing up as they get older.

If he chooses to sit, he will need to be shown how to push his penis down so that the pee hits the toilet bowl or goes into the potty rather than over the floor. A potty with a built-in splashguard will help prevent this happening, but your son may become dependent on the guard rather than learning to keep his penis pointing down. Always be careful if you buy a potty with a detachable splashguard as your son may catch or scrape his penis and hurt himself. If you have this type of potty, it may be worth removing the deflector before use.

Little boys often start learning to pee sitting down, but most want to be just like their fathers or friends and will soon have a go doing it standing up.

As a single mum I found it difficult to toilet train my son, Sam. Because there was no male role model for him to copy he insisted on sitting on the toilet to pee rather than standing up. I worried that he would be laughed at when he went to nursery for not doing what the other boys did. Then a friend told me about putting targets in the toilet bowl for him to aim at. Once peeing into the bowl became such fun he never wanted to pee sitting down again.

Learning to stand

If your son is happy sitting down to urinate, don't rush into having him stand up. Wait until he has developed sufficient control. On the other hand, if he wants to use a regular toilet to pee into, don't force him into using a potty.

He'll certainly want to stand up when he reaches pre-school age as he'll probably try to copy his dad or other boys from his play group. Often, children learn best by imitation, so someone, preferably his dad or an older male, will have to show him how to stand up in front of the toilet and aim into the bowl before urinating. If you can't involve a male adult, your son will still learn to stand, but it may take a little longer.

Once your son understands the process, it's just a matter of practising until this new skill becomes a habit. Make sure, of course, that you teach your son to lift the toilet seat before urinating and, once up, that it remains securely in place. Injuries can be caused by falling seats. He'll also need to be taught to 'shake dry' afterwards without getting drips all over the floor and his pants.

Perfecting his aim

Standing up and peeing on target is a tricky manoeuvre for a little boy to perfect. Get your son to direct his penis toward the drain hole before he starts to pee. Getting it right can take plenty of practise – up to a year or more before the floor and walls remain completely free of splashes. Keep a sturdy stepstool nearby; this not only makes it easier for your boy to access the toilet by himself, but will also help him aim more effectively into the bowl.

Toilet targets

Your child can practise getting his pee into the toilet bowl, and also have lots of fun, by trying to hit a floating target. Drop 'O'-shaped cereal or small pieces of torn up toilet paper into the bowl for him to aim at. Manufactured biodegradable 'toilet targets' are also available.

potty training girls

There is no real physical or anatomical reason why girls should be easier and quicker to potty train than boys, yet the fact remains that in many cases this is true. One reason may be that mothers, or female carers, are usually the main people involved in potty training, and it is easier for girls to imitate them than it is for boys. Also girls mature more quickly than boys – they reach puberty on average a year or two earlier. It may just be that pre-school-age boys tend to be more difficult than girls of the same age, and that being quicker to potty train is just part of girls' generally more mature behaviour pattern.

Toilet tactics

Just as a boy makes his own decision about standing or sitting, your daughter will make it clear whether she prefers using a potty or sitting on the toilet seat like mum. If she decides on the toilet, you'll need to use a special children's toilet seat (see p.51) and a stepping stool to help her climb onto the seat.

Getting into the right position

You may find that your daughter sits too far forward so her pee wets her panties. Show her how to sit far enough back on the seat to get the

Little girls often pee on their underwear by mistake, and may find it easier to take their panties off completely before using the potty.

CHILD'S PLAY

pee in the toilet, and help her slide her pants right down to her ankles so they're safely out of harm's way. Once she feels comfortable sitting on the toilet she'll find a position that allows her to pee into the toilet bowl without any problems. If she prefers to use the potty, and providing she's able to pull her pants up and down herself, she should be able to manage without too much help.

You won't always have a potty or toilet close at hand when your child has the urge to go, and she may sometimes need to pee outdoors. This isn't a problem for boys, but girls need to keep their feet and clothes well clear as they squat. Holding your little girl as she squats will make it easier for her to stay in the right position.

Learning her limits

Sometimes little girls try to copy their fathers, brothers or their friends at child care by trying to pee standing up. It may make a bit of mess, but she'll soon realize it doesn't work. Watching her mother or another girl use the toilet will help her get the right idea.

Wiping the right way

You should teach your little girl to wipe herself dry from front to back – that is, towards the anus. Wiping the wrong way risks transferring bacteria from her anus to her urinary tract, which may result in an infection – one reason why girls of potty-training age are more likely to get urinary tract infections than boys or older girls (see p.30 for advice on symptoms and treatment). You will probably need to continue helping your child to wipe herself for some time – young children seldom do a very thorough job – but you should encourage her to attempt it herself.

good hygiene habits

Children need to learn about hygiene as soon as they start using the potty or toilet – good habits gained young will be a lifetime benefit. But while hygiene is important, don't become obsessive – your child may try to retain his bowel movements in an effort to avoid any fuss.

Children need to learn a range of bathroom skills, from regular bathing to teeth cleaning. Good toilet hygiene habits such as wiping, flushing the toilet and washing his hands should be taught as a part of these routines. Your child may find all this a lot to learn at once. One way to make sure that he doesn't forget the important points is to make him a special chart. Include boxes for washing, flushing and wiping, as well as anything else he needs to do regularly, such as washing his face or brushing his teeth.

Wiping

Getting clean after using the toilet may be something of a challenge for your child, and you will have to assist him at first. Parents usually need to help their children with wiping until they are about five years old, but the sooner he gets the hang of it the better.

Some children are fascinated by flushing, and will do it as often as you allow, others are more fearful and need to slowly overcome their fears.

Bath tissues have a cloth-like consistency that makes cleaning easier. Pre-moistened, flushable wipes are gentle on the skin, easy for your child to use and may be more effective than regular toilet paper when cleaning after a poop.

Flushing

When you first start potty training, you may find that your toddler becomes upset at the sight of his much-praised efforts being flushed down the toilet. If this is the case, empty the potty or flush the toilet once he has left the bathroom. Another reason for your child being upset at flushing is the noise it makes. He may be fearful of the toilet because he is worried about falling in and being flushed away himself. He will gradually overcome these fears and when he does you should encourage him to flush the toilet himself. Once your child feels confident enough to do this you can help him to empty his potty into the toilet and then allow him to flush it. Encourage your child to close the toilet lid before flushing so that he avoids contact with germs that may spray up.

Some children are much more enthusiastic about flushing and may be fascinated by the noise it makes. You may even find it difficult to stop your child flushing the toilet again and again. If this is the case, don't allow him to use the flush whenever he wants – try to keep it as an incentive to encourage him to use the toilet properly. If he really can't be dissuaded from overusing the flush, consider fitting a child-proof attachment to your toilet.

Hygiene habits such as hand washing and teeth cleaning are important to learn while young so that they come naturally to your child.

With both boys and girls, encourage gentle wiping. If a child wipes sensitive skin too roughly, it may become irritated. You'll also need to show your child how much toilet paper to use – left to their own devices, children tend to make over-enthusiastic swipes at the roll and clog up the toilet. Girls should be taught to wipe from front to back to prevent germs being transferred to the urinary tract. Little boys will also need to be taught to 'shake dry'.

You can help encourage your child's bathroom independence with products that are gentle on his sensitive skin, but also are strong and absorbent.

Dirty doll

One way of helping your toddler perfect her wiping technique is to get her to practise on a wipeable toy or doll. Smear the doll's bottom with chocolate or jam and let your child give it a good clean once the toy has 'used the potty'. Point out any lingering stains but make sure you give your child plenty of praise for a job well done.

Washing

Hand washing is very important, as germs can be easily transferred from the toilet to your child's mouth. You should explain to your toddler that germs are much too tiny to see, and even if his hands look clean they may still be present on his skin. Don't overdo your lecture – your don't want to make your child germ-obsessed!

One of the easiest ways to teach your child to wash his hands properly is to wash yours at the same time. Use soap and pay particular attention to drying your hands afterwards. Try saying a rhyme or counting up to ten each time your child washes his hands, so that he gets an idea of how long he needs to wash them. Your child may enjoy having his own special soap to wash his hands with – you can get him one in the shape of his favourite animal.

Poop play

Children are often fascinated by their bodily products, and may try to touch or play with their pee or poop. Telling your toddler not to play with his poop can sometimes make him even more convinced that it must be special. Explain to him that pee and poop contain lots of germs, but don't make a big deal about it. Instead, try to divert his attention onto something else. Your child will soon grow out of his unhygienic habits.

learning control

Some children learn control quicker than others, but providing your child is physically and emotionally mature enough when you start, you should find he'll soon start to get the hang of things – although he may continue to have accidents for some time. It is thought that bowel control is easier to achieve than control over the bladder, but there are no hard and fast rules about this. Although your child's muscles allow him to 'hold on' to a bowel movement for longer than urine, the need to go may not be so pronounced and he may find it more difficult to recognize the signs. It is also possible for a child to achieve simultaneous bladder and bowel control – this is more likely to occur in children who are already quite mature when they begin potty training.

Whichever one your child learns first, what is important is that he has control of one of these functions. Learning to control the other will occur in time – there is no point in pressuring your child to achieve it before he is ready.

Night-time bladder control

Once bladder control has been learned, your child will get through the day with few accidents, but is still likely to wake up wet. Many children do not achieve 100 per cent night-time control until several months after learning to stay dry in the day. Of course, some children achieve dryness at night at the same time, or very close to the time they achieve daytime dryness. Whichever your child does is quite normal.

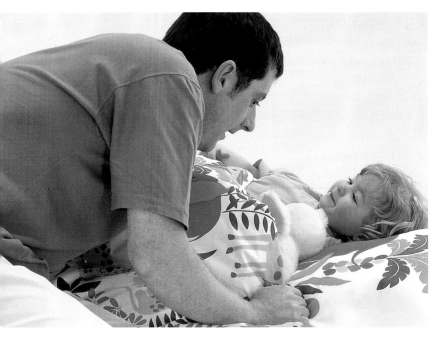

Many children take a long time to learn to stay dry at night – around 20 per cent of five-year-olds still wet their beds.

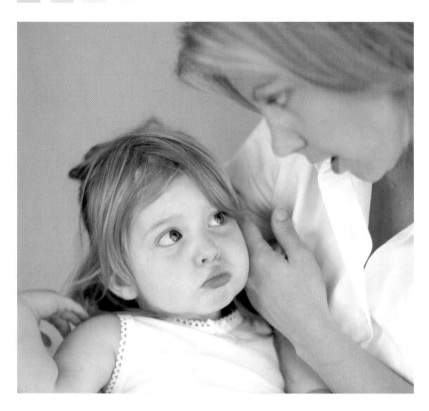

Most children will still have the occasional accident now and then. This can be very discouraging for a child, so it is important to offer plenty of comfort and reassurance.

Accidents will happen

It would be unrealistic to think that your child will never wet or poop himself again once he's got the hang of using the potty or toilet. Sometimes it is just a question of timing – such as when he doesn't manage to get to the bathroom quickly enough. On other occasions it may be forgetfulness – he may be too busy in his own world and not respond to the sensation of needing to go. Try to remember that accidents play an important part in potty training because they help your child realize what happens when he feels the need to pee or poop.

Giving reassurance

Your child may feel ashamed or embarrassed when he has an accident. This will only discourage him and may set him back. Try to express calm reassurance that it isn't anything to

HANDY **HINTS...**

- Keep some spare pairs of pants, trousers or tights where your child can reach them, so that she can get replacements for herself.

- If convenient, suggest that she puts the wet or dirty clothes in the laundry basket or washing machine herself.

- Put her in plastic sandals or let her run around in bare feet, so that her shoes or slippers don't come in contact with pee or poop.

- Keep a cloth and bucket ready, so that you can clean up after an accident with a minimum of fuss.

PREPARING FOR ACCIDENTS

be concerned about and remind him gently that next time he should tell you that he needs the potty or wants to go to the bathroom. Don't tell him that he has to remember to go every time – this will only put pressure on him, which will have a negative effect. By giving him lots of reassurance he will begin to realize that this is something he can achieve, even though he has accidents occasionally.

Power struggles

It is quite natural to feel upset, even angry, when your child has frequent accidents, but these emotions are often counter-productive. Some children may be frightened by anger and may continue to wet or soil as a result of this fear. Other children enjoy being the focus of attention, even if that attention is total disapproval. After all, this is one of the few areas of life where parents can't force their child to do what they want – if your child decides to wet his underwear, there is nothing you can do to stop him. Your child may enjoy the fact that this gives him a certain amount of power over you, and the more angry you get with him, the more control he has over your emotions.

Defusing the situation

If you feel anger or frustration over mopping up for the tenth time that day, try talking to your child about how you feel rather than resorting to yelling or even smacking. Explain that all the extra work has made you feel tired and rather cross, and that it would be better for both of you if he used the potty in the future. This way he knows how you are feeling, but doesn't have the satisfaction of being able to make you lose your temper. By not fighting over accidents, you are preventing your child from using them as a means of getting your attention.

Be prepared

Rather than being upset by your child's accidents, be prepared for them so that you can minimize their effect. Pee is easy to mop up off hard floors, and carpets and upholstery can be cleaned with a regular household cleaner. Poop is rather messier to deal with. If your child poops in his pants you may find it easiest to clean him up in the shower or bathtub. Remove his soiled clothing and calmly explain that next time he needs to poop he should tell you so he can do it in the potty or the toilet.

Once you have cleaned your child up, try to get him to sit on the potty or toilet for a minute or so. Tell him that he should see if there is any more to come. This helps reinforce the connection of pee or poop with using the potty.

staying dry at night

If your toddler doesn't achieve night-time dryness at around the same time as she becomes dry during the day, she is not alone. Most children won't be regularly dry at night until several months after this. After all, getting to the toilet on time is a lot easier for your child when feeling bright and awake than when half asleep.

How you cope with dry days and wet nights is very much up to you. Some parents are happy to put their toddler in a nappy at night, others are concerned that this gives a child mixed messages. How can a child understand that it is all right to wet her nappy at night but it is not acceptable to do so during the day?

It is important to remember that your child doesn't wet herself at night on purpose or because she is lazy. Children's bodies develop at different rates and physically she may not be sufficiently developed to last through the night without passing urine. Or it may be that she sleeps very deeply and doesn't feel the sensation of needing to pee. The bladder, once full, automatically empties itself, just as it did when she was a baby.

If your child is still having accidents during the day or pees every couple of hours, she is not ready for night-time dryness and will be happier in nappies at night.

Many children don't achieve night-time dryness until at least six months after they are dry during the day.

Encouraging dry nights

Once your child has had a few dry nights, you can try leaving her nappy off. Some children even ask not to wear nappies at night. Don't be concerned about returning to nappies if this doesn't work – it may take several attempts before you achieve success. Putting a waterproof sheet over the mattress or placing an absorbent disposable nappy-style cover on the bed will prevent the mattress becoming soaked and smelly, and minimize your washing. You could even use two layers of waterproof and regular sheets on the bed, so you can simply pull off the wet sheets and still have a dry layer underneath.

Using the toilet at night

Not all children have strong enough bladder muscles to keep them dry through the night and your child may need to get up in the night to use the potty or toilet. If your child has successfully learnt to use the toilet during the day, she should learn to use it at night, too, in time. Putting a potty in the bedroom for your child to use in the night may be helpful. The downside to this is that urine can make the room smell, and there is a risk that your child may knock the full potty over when she gets out of bed in the morning.

Make sure your child's bedroom is warm enough, so she doesn't mind leaving the comfort of her cozy bed, and think about providing a nightlight so that the darkness in her room doesn't seem quite so frightening. Restricting the amount of fluid your child drinks before bedtime will mean she produces less pee during the night, but makes the pee she does produce more concentrated, and this won't help with her bladder control. Don't restrict her drinks so much that she goes to bed thirsty. A small, pre-bedtime drink of a non-stimulating liquid such as milk or water won't have any effect on night-time bed-wetting.

Waking and lifting

One solution that many parents adopt for night-time bed-wetting involves getting the child up in the night and sitting her on the toilet or potty to pass urine. This can be very tiresome for parents and some experts argue that this makes children dependent on their parents to wake them up, so that they don't learn to take responsibility for getting themselves up when they feel the need to go. Despite this, it can be useful when you first start as a way to introduce your child to the concept of waking up during the night when she feels the urge.

WHEN CAN YOU EXPECT DRY NIGHTS?

Approximate % of bed-wetters

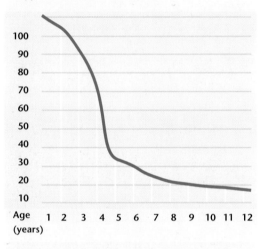

This chart shows the approximate percentage of children who wet the bed at different ages. Doctors do not usually consider bed-wetting to be a problem until at least five years of age.

Lifting sleeping toddlers

If your toddler becomes upset when you wake her, lifting can become a rather stressful tactic. It may be tempting to lift your child and take her to the bathroom without properly waking her, but experts say the child needs to be awake so she is aware of what is going on. Taking a sleeping toddler to the bathroom may save you a wet bed but it won't actually help with night-time control. Indeed this kind of lifting may even delay the age at which your child develops control, since she will have learnt to sleep right through the urge to urinate.

Be aware

You need to be aware of how wetting herself at night affects your child. She may feel discouraged and ashamed, which will harm her self-esteem. Don't make a big deal out of changing her wet sheets, and rather than becoming cross about her accident explain to your child that this is quite normal and that she will become dry at night once she has grown up a bit more. As in all aspects of potty training, it is important to remain positive and supportive, since criticism is often counter-productive.

Night-time bowel movements

It is extremely unusual for a child who is potty trained during the day to poop in her bed during the night. However, it is not uncommon for a child to do a poop once she has had her nappy put on at night, or in the morning before you have a chance to take the nappy off. This may be because the feeling of poop in her nappy gives her a sense of familiarity or security.

coping with setbacks

Few parents are lucky enough to achieve potty training success without experiencing any setbacks. It can be extremely frustrating to have a child who persistently wets the bed or who regresses after a period of dryness, but the best way to cope with training problems is to stay calm and positive, and to try to understand why they have occurred in the first place.

Regression

This can occur at any time and is often associated with stress or illness. Your child may have been dry for a number of weeks and then suddenly start to have accident after accident. This may take you by surprise and is very likely to make you feel upset and bewildered.

Start by trying to work out what is upsetting your child. It may be something obvious, such as starting nursery school or a change in her caregiver, or it could just be a change in routine or some upset at home. Whatever the cause, you must reassure your child and be patient and understanding about both the cause of the stress and the accidents. Scolding or putting pressure on your child to remember to use the toilet will only add to the problem and make your child more nervous and upset.

You may consider putting your toddler back into nappies. There are no hard and fast rules about this and your decision should be based on your understanding of your child and your own tolerance for coping with accidents. It is worth bearing in mind that periods of regression are usually only temporary, lasting for a short period

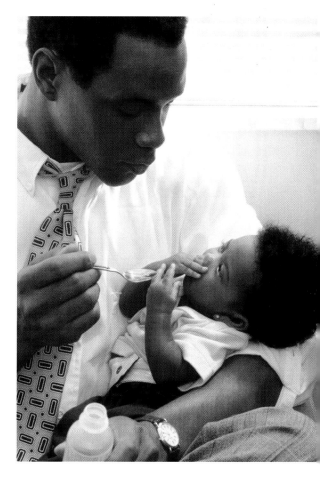

A period of illness can sometimes disrupt the potty-training process or cause a previously potty-trained child to regress.

of time. Longer periods of regression may occur, especially if your child has been unwell. Diarrhoea and urinary tract infections can result in frequent accidents, and you may want to put your child into training pants while he is unwell. This will allow him to continue to be independent and to use the potty, but will help to contain any mess.

Persistent bed-wetting

It is very common for children to continue to wet the bed for some time after gaining control during the day, and if your child is under the age of six it is probably best to wait and see if things improve with age. But some children continue to have problems with bed-wetting (nocturnal enuresis) well past their sixth birthday, and as many as 5 per cent of 10-year-olds have difficulty staying dry at night.

Although bed-wetting is not harmful in itself, it can be extremely frustrating for parents and children alike. Older children who continue to wet the bed may be ashamed of their lack of control or find that it prevents them from taking part in activities such as school trips or stays over at friends' houses. Parents will certainly soon tire of having to change wet and smelly bedclothes.

Understanding bed-wetting

The causes of persistent bed-wetting are still not completely understood and there is often a combination of factors involved. There may be some physical or developmental problem – a child may simply have slow physical maturation, or he may have some physical abnormality such as particularly small bladder or some type of muscle weakness or bladder instability. A very small minority of children have a deficiency in antidiuretic hormone (ADH), a hormone that

WHAT ROLE DOES GENETICS PLAY?

Bed-wetting often runs in families. Studies suggest children are much more likely to have problems staying dry during the night if one or both of their parents were once bed-wetters too.

If you or your partner suffered from problems when younger, do let your child know. It will be immensely reassuring to hear a parent or family member once wet the bed too, just like them.

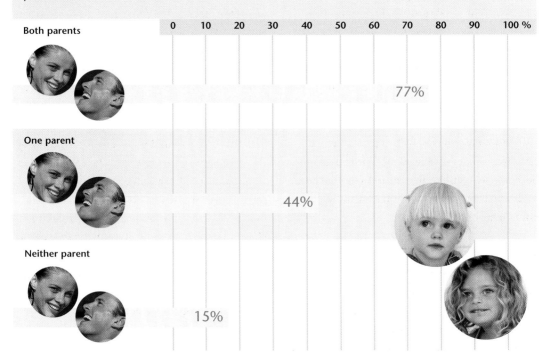

| | 0 | 10 | 20 | 30 | 40 | 50 | 60 | 70 | 80 | 90 | 100 % |

Both parents

77%

One parent

44%

Neither parent

15%

reduces the amount of urine produced at night. Physical and medical problems can be treated with various techniques, so you should always seek professional advice.

Some children who have problems with persistent bed-wetting are particularly heavy sleepers – although there are usually other factors involved, too. In some cases – although by no means all – bed-wetting may be linked to stress or worry. This is particularly likely to be a factor in cases where a child has had a period of dry nights before regressing. In such an instance it is particularly important not to scold your child, since this will only make things worse. If you suspect your child is unhappy and his bed-wetting persists you should consider seeking professional help.

Treating bed-wetting

There are no hard and fast rules regarding the best way to treat a persistent bed-wetter. The majority of children will eventually grow out of their problems, and support and reassurance may be all that's needed. However exasperated you feel, try to remain positive – star charts can be a good way of reinforcing positive behaviour.

You could also encourage your child to wait as long as possible before urinating during the day. This will stretch the bladder, allowing it to hold more urine which will help to delay the need to urinate in the night. When your child does urinate, get him to stop and start the flow as this will strengthen the sphincter muscles that hold the urine in.

Conditioning

It may also be possible to condition your child into waking during the night to use the toilet. One way to do this is by rousing him at a set time each night so that he gets used to waking up to use the toilet (for more information on lifting,

see p.75). Another option is some sort of bed-wetting alarm, usually consisting of a sensor placed under the sheet to wake your child if he wets the bed, so he learns to associate the need to urinate with waking up.

Medications

The risk with medications is that you are treating the symptoms of bed-wetting rather than the cause. Your child may come to rely on them rather than learn to control himself. Because of this, medications are not usually prescribed to children except in combination with other types of treatment. If your child does have an ADH deficiency, your doctor may wish to prescribe an antidiuretic medication to decrease urine production during the night.

WATCH POINT...

In a small minority of children who wet the bed, the accidents are a symptom of a urinary tract infection (see p.30). If bed-wetting is accompanied by any of the following symptoms, particularly if your child has started to wet the bed after a period of night-time dryness, your should take your child to see a doctor or other healthcare provider to rule out an infection as the cause:

- Fever
- Abdominal pain
- More frequent urination than is usual
- Pain during urination
- Blood in urine

Refusal to go

Your child may be perfectly happy to pee in the potty but refuse point-blank to do a poop in it. As a result he may become constipated or soil his pants. In some cases, a child may even deposit his stools in a corner or closet. You may feel that your child is deliberately provoking you. A more likely reason for this behaviour is that he is just finding it hard to cope with all the demands of potty training at one time. He may also feel that you are too controlling and that he wants to have control over his bodily functions himself.

Constipation

Refusal to go may be complicated by constipation. A child who holds in his stools for a prolonged period may end up with the faeces becoming impacted in the rectum. This leads to discomfort and even pain, making your child even more reluctant to poop. Don't ignore this, as the problem may well get worse before it gets better; ask your doctor for advice. See p. 32 for more information on constipation.

Reluctance to do a bowel movement in the potty is not uncommon, but can be hard to deal with. Try not to get angry with your child or you may make the problem worse.

Encopresis

This occurs when a child retains his bowel movements over a long period, so that his stools become hard and impacted (packed together inside the rectum and difficult to pass). This may lead to nerve damage so that your child can no longer feel what is happening and has no control over his soiling. Loose, liquid stools leak out around these solid, impacted stools, so that your child's underpants become soiled, maybe several times a day. A child who suffers from encopresis needs help because soiling is embarrassing and the impacted stools could, if left untreated, cause damage to the colon.

6 Special situations

When it comes to potty training, there are certain special situations that will require particular consideration. Perhaps you have just had a new baby and your toddler is jealous of the new arrival; maybe you and your partner are separated but share in the care of your child; you might have boisterous twins or a disabled child to cope with; or you may simply want to know how best to manage your still-training toddler when away from home or on holiday. These situations, although by no means out of the ordinary, require you to think hard about the best approach to keep your child on track and make potty training a success.

away from home

Once training has started, you will need to be able to cope with situations outside your home. It is likely to be a while before your child is confident enough to ask for – or prepared to use – public facilities, so you will probably have a period of taking a potty out and about with you.

Journeys

If you are going on a car trip, you will need to be prepared for frequent stops, so allow some extra time when planning the journey. Make sure your child uses the potty or toilet before you set off.

Carry the potty in the car so it is easily accessible, along with wipes, toilet paper and a change of clothes in case of accidents. Cut down on drinks both before and during the journey, and avoid altogether those that stimulate your child's bladder, such as fizzy drinks. If you travel a lot, you may want to invest in a travel potty with a lid so that you can keep any poop in the potty to dispose of when convenient.

Travelling by aeroplane should not cause too many problems, providing your child can be persuaded to use the available toilets. If your child prefers to use a potty, it may be useful to

Long car journeys with young children can be very stressful. If your child isn't happy using a regular toilet, take a travel potty – the one shown here folds flat for easy storage and takes a disposable liner that can be tied up after use.

carry one in your hand luggage for her to use in the plane toilet. Trains and boats usually have toilets on board, but these can sometimes be rather unpleasant to use. Having your own potty on hand, along with wipes, will make the journey more comfortable for your child.

Childcare

Many nurseries and childcare centres expect children to be at least partially trained before they will accept them at the beginning of a new term. Caregivers may have a large number of children to look after and coping with nappies would not be practical. This does sometimes put pressure on parents to get their children clean and dry before they are properly ready.

Fears and concerns

Even when your child has learned to use the bathroom, be prepared for accidents when she starts at nursery. At first it will all be very strange for her, especially if she is being separated from you for the first time, and she'll have to learn a lot of new things quickly. Your child may be expected to use the bathroom without being reminded, which she might not understand. She may be nervous about going on her own, or worried because the toilet flush makes a different noise to the one at home. She may not be able to reach the light switch, or be shy about using the toilet when there are so many people around. Or she may simply be feeling stressed by all the new experiences. Find out what is worrying your child and help her overcome her fears, and the accidents should soon stop.

Distractions

The most likely reason for your child to have the occasional accident at the nursery or the childcare centre is simply that she's too busy to

Children are easily disoriented by the unfamiliar, so be prepared for your child's potty training to regress slightly on holidays.

notice the need to go. If your child is very focused and keen to learn, she may not want to go to the bathroom in case she might miss something. Or she may rush to the toilet and be so eager to hurry back to what she is doing that she gets pee all over her clothes by mistake. Provide her with a change of clothes each day and ask her caregiver to supervise visits to the bathroom until she can manage by herself.

coping with a new baby

The arrival of a new baby can cause a toddler to regress in his behaviour. Although your child may seem delighted with his new brother or sister, he may resent all the fuss being made over the baby. He may feel it is unfair that this interloper takes up so much of your time and may start wetting himself in an effort to get back your attention and reclaim his status as the baby of the family.

Give it time

Allow your child time to adjust to the new arrival. Reassure him that although his new brother or sister is taking up a lot of your time,

you still love him, and explain to him that he has his own special place in the family. Boost his confidence by telling him what an important role he has as a big brother, and that part of this new grown-up role involves remembering to use the bathroom. Explain that the new baby requires a lot of work, and tell him how glad you are that he is so grown up.

Having a new baby around can make your child feel very insecure about her status in the family. Try to get her involved in looking after the new arrival, and emphasize how important she is to you.

Having tantrums and wetting himself are classic ways for a toddler to grab the limelight back from a baby brother or sister. He may feel that even a negative response is better than nothing.

Stay calm

Try to be matter of fact about any accidents, get him to help you clean them up and don't scold, shame or punish him. If you respond with anger or tears he is likely to continue wetting or dirtying himself just to get this kind of emotional response from you. It can be exciting for a child to discover that he can reduce you to tears by simply wetting the floor.

Talk to your child

Try to get your child to tell you exactly how he feels about the new baby, and let him know that it is fine for him to feel cross or jealous at first. If your toddler is able to verbalize his resentment, he is less likely to express his feelings in other ways, such as having tantrums or wetting his pants. It is important that your child does not bottle up his perfectly natural frustration at no longer being the focus of the family's attention.

Practical solutions

If you feel you cannot cope with a new baby and a toddler who frequently wets or dirties himself, you may want to consider putting him back in nappies or training pants for a while. Don't give up on the potty training though, and keep to the same routine you used previously. You are likely to find that within a few weeks your toddler is using the bathroom without any problems.

coping with twins

Although the idea of having to train two – or more – babies at once may seem daunting, the techniques for training twins are essentially the same as for a single child. It will, of course, be more difficult to give twins the individual attention that potty training requires, so try to enlist some help before you start. Perhaps your partner or a relative could lend a hand, at least for the first few days.

Keeping track of two curious, nappyless kids at once can be a messy business, so wait until you are sure they are ready.

Be prepared

Training two children means twice as many accidents to clean up and twice as much laundry, so it is important to choose a time when you feel physically and emotionally ready for all the extra work this can involve.

Before you begin, take a look at the readiness checklist on page 40 to check that both children show signs of being physically and emotionally mature enough. You may even want to leave training until the children have reached the age of three, as their increased maturity will help make the whole process less stressful.

Treating twins as individuals

Don't assume that your children will always want to do everything together – twins sometimes struggle to define their identity as individuals, and this holds true during potty training too. You will need to invest in more than one potty so that they have each got one of their own – training is difficult enough without trying to persuade two children to share a potty. Let your twins personalize their potties with stickers or name labels to give them a sense of personal ownership.

If only one twin appears to be ready to begin potty training, you may want to start training the children individually, or you may prefer to wait until they are both sufficiently mature and you can start them together. Training them separately may make it easier for each child to focus on their own body and their personal progress.

> ### TRAINING FOR TWO
>
> My daughter was potty trained at the age of two, and it really wasn't a big deal, so when it came to training my twin boys I took the same approach – sitting them on the potty at regular intervals. James got the hang of it quite quickly, but Michael took longer and absolutely refused to do a poop in the potty for about three months. I think he was jealous of his brother's success. Although I had to do a lot of chasing around after them for the first few weeks, training the twins wasn't a lot harder than training my daughter.

Learning by example

If you embark on potty training the children together, you may find that one twin makes progress faster than the other. This can actually be helpful, as the child who is progressing fastest will help to encourage the other twin, and the slower learner will soon want to imitate his

Some twins like to do everything at the same time, including potty training; other twins will crawl in opposite directions at the very first opportunity.

brother or sister. It is quite normal for one child to achieve success before the other, but don't be tempted to use the successful twin's achievement to belittle the other child when he has an accident, as this may prolong the time it takes to get the slower child trained.

when parents live apart

If you and your partner are separated, but share in the care of your child, it is beneficial to coordinate your potty-training strategy. This doesn't mean that both of you have to follow the same routine – indeed your child may benefit from a flexible approach to training. But it is important to keep each other informed of his progress and to be aware of any setbacks, as these could be linked to the way you behave towards each other. Any arguments or disagreements will distress your child, and this may be reflected in his behaviour, making him harder to potty train.

Getting started

If your child lives with you most of the time and sees his other parent only at weekends, it will be best for him to begin potty training with you, in familiar surroundings. Once the process has been started, it then becomes easier for it to be continued by his other parent.

If possible, have a routine that both you and your partner can follow easily, so that your child doesn't become confused by different training methods. Having the same style of potty or toilet seat in each home will make your child feel more comfortable about using it.

Talk to your child about the potty-training routine he has with your ex-partner, so you don't confuse him by taking a different approach.

A chart that records your child's progress will give him a chance to show each of you his achievements. The chart can be filled in by whichever parent he is with at the time. This way neither of you miss out on his successes. For this to work you will need to agree about what your child has to do to earn a sticker or star for his chart, and whether you give him rewards.

Offer reassurance

Sometimes, a child is more willing to cooperate with a parent that he sees less frequently. However, he may also be more upset about any accidents he has and worried about causing disappointment. He may even think that having accidents will in some way affect his relationship with the parent he sees less often. It is important to reassure your child, so he understands that any accidents he may have in no way affect the love you both have for him.

Be flexible

If your child goes to visit your ex-partner only occasionally and the time they have together is spent going out and having fun, their activities together may be disrupted by potty training. It is better to be flexible about training on these occasions. Let your child wear training pants while he's out, rather than trying to insist that he always follows his potty routine. Once he is more confident about getting to the toilet on time he'll be able to enjoy his days out without having any accidents.

Don't be competitive

It's easy for potty training to become an area of competition, especially if you have a difficult or acrimonious relationship with your ex-partner. If one of you views potty-training success as a sign of better parenting, then for the sake of your child the other parent should try to stay out of

Reassure your child that although you do want him to learn control, accidents will not have any affect on your feelings for him.

the competition. It is important that your potty-training strategies do not contradict each other, and that your child does not become confused by competing approaches. You need to protect your toddler from any tension between you and your ex-partner, which will have only a negative affect on his behaviour.

children with disabilities

If you have a child with a physical or mental disability, potty training can be an especially important step. Gaining control of her bladder and bowels will greatly increase your child's independence and give her a feeling of responsibility. Toilet training can be a slow process for a disabled child, but don't let yourself get overwhelmed – with specialist help and plenty of patience it should definitely be something you can achieve.

Learning difficulties

Children with learning difficulties may need to start potty training later, and may take considerably longer than other children to become clean and dry. However, the methods used are the same as with any other child. You will need to be very patient and you may want to involve other caregivers on a daily basis. If your child spends time in a special care home, you will need to discuss the training methods that are used by her caregivers so that you can adopt the same procedures in your own home.

Physical disabilities

A few children – such as those with spinal cord injuries or spina bifida – may never develop voluntary control over the bladder or bowel, but most children with physical disabilities have normal muscle control. They may, however, have problems that physically prevent them getting to the potty or toilet in time. Even a minor degree of clumsiness, caused by an impairment, can make coping with clothing and sitting on the

Teaching your child control can be a frustrating process for you both – but success will make all the effort seem worthwhile.

Jessica has Down's syndrome, and I had been warned that she might be difficult to potty train. She seemed ready at about two-and-a-half so I started sitting her on the potty first thing every morning and after every mealtime. She soon got the idea and was dry during the day within a couple of months, and by the time she was three years old she was dry at night, too.

and her sense of achievement when she succeeds will make all the difficulties you encountered along the way seem unimportant.

Blind and sight-impaired children will also have obvious problems with potty training and using the toilet. Your child will need special teaching to overcome these obstacles, but as she gets older and becomes more independent she will learn how best to manage the difficulties.

Getting help

Talk to your child's healthcare providers about the best toilet-training methods to use and ask for their help and support. They may be able to refer you to a continence specialist – usually a trained nurse who specializes in this area.

Charities and support groups concerned with disabilities often have useful information and may be able to tell you about aids for incontinence suitable for older children. They may also be able to put you in touch with other parents who have been through similar experiences to the ones you are encountering. You will find it helpful to talk to people who have been through the same difficulties you are now facing.

Give yourself a break

Caring for a child with a disability can be exhausting, without the added stress of trying to potty train. Involve others in her training routine and allow yourself time to relax. You may even find that your child responds better to a person who is not so involved in her day-to-day care, and will be more willing to cooperate with any training methods that have been suggested.

potty or toilet difficult. You may need to wait until your child is much older before you can consider potty training. Your child will need a lot of extra help as she copes with her disability while learning this new skill.

Before you begin, speak to your doctor or occupational therapist about purchasing special aids or equipment to help your child use the toilet. There's a wide choice of equipment available, from specialized potty chairs (usually custom-made to your child's requirements), to grab bars that fit on either side of the toilet and special toilet supports. Even if your child is wheelchair-bound, there are special props that will help her to use the toilet.

Sight and sound

A child who has hearing difficulties is likely to have problems with language and communication. This makes it hard for her to understand and cooperate with you about potty training. In time she will learn what it is you are asking her to do

commonly asked questions

? My daughter was premature and weighed only 1.8 kg (4 pounds) at birth. Now she's three and has no problems at all, apart from the fact that she isn't potty trained. Could the fact that she was premature have an effect on her ability to control her bladder and bowels?

There is some research that suggests that babies born weighing less that 2.5 kg (5½ pounds) take longer to become dry than babies who were of average, or above average weight at birth.

? At what age should I be concerned about my child not being toilet trained?

If your child has not achieved daytime control by three-and-a-half to four years of age, and is not dry at night by the age of six, he may have a physical problem. You should consult your doctor to rule out any physical causes. Your doctor may also suggest that you see a child psychologist who can help your child overcome any other difficulties.

? When should I expect my child to be able to wipe his own bottom properly?

This is a skill that needs to be taught and then practised over and over again. Many mothers are still wiping their children's bottoms long after the children have learned to use the toilet by themselves. Aim to have your child independently wiping his bottom by the time he starts school. By this age he should also be able to wash his hands properly and flush the toilet.

? My partner gets very cross with our little girl when she has an accident. He thinks smacking her will make her use the toilet to avoid further punishment. Is he right?

Smacking is never appropriate when guiding a child toward learning a new skill, and is certainly not the right way to go about achieving potty training. In fact, smacks on the bottom actually delay the process because they humiliate the child and build up resentment between parent and child.

? My son won't eat any fruit or vegetables and has severe bouts of constipation because of the lack of fibre in his diet. I have been told that I must make him eat more healthily, but he simply refuses to eat things he doesn't like. What can I do?

? My son has been dry for several weeks, and takes himself off to the bathroom to pee in the toilet without any help from me. But he absolutely refuses to poop anywhere other than in a nappy. What should I do?

It's important not to force-feed a child, but there are ways of introducing fibre into his diet that he may find acceptable.

Vegetables are sometimes more tempting raw rather than cooked – try cutting fresh, crunchy vegetables into sticks which your child can dip into his favourite sauce. Or you could try giving him vegetable soup made with beans and other pulses. Most children will eat cereal in the morning, so you could offer cereals made with whole grains, or try porridge. Wholemeal bread is a good source of fibre and most children will eat it if it is made into bread-soldiers and topped with their favourite spread. He may like to try dried fruit snacks such as bananas or apricot.

Be inventive and make mealtimes fun occasions so that your child looks forward to eating. Do remember that your child also needs to drink plenty of fluids – lack of fluid can also cause constipation.

Remember that urine training and bowel training are two different processes. Some children learn them almost simultaneously, others learn to control one before the other. If your child is asking for a nappy when he needs to poop you should let him wear one. Refusing may lead to bowel retention and a power struggle. He has already shown he can use the toilet, so you should trust him to decide for himself when he is ready to poop in the toilet.

index

A

accidents, 72–3, 74
  in childcare, 83
  new babies and, 85
  punishment, 92
  regression, 77
adult-led training, 43–4
air travel, 82–3
alarms, bed-wetting, 79
allergy, food, 34
ammonia, 8, 28
anal fissures, 15, 34
antibiotics, 15, 30
antidiuretic hormone (ADH), 78–9
anus, 11

B

babies, new, 84–5
barrier cream, 26, 28
bed-wetting, 74–6, 78–9
bladder, 6–7
  infections, 9
bladder control, 36–7
  at night, 71, 74–6
blood: in stools, 34
  in urine, 31
bottle-feeding, 12, 13, 32
bowel control, 36–7, 71
  at night, 76
bowel movements *see* stools
boys: changing nappies, 25
  potty-training, 64–5
breast-feeding, 8, 12, 13, 28, 34

C

candidal nappy rash, 28
car trips, 82
caregivers, 55–6, 83
charts, star, 63, 79, 89
childcare, 55–6, 83
child-led training, 43
cloth nappies, 8, 20–3
clothes, 61
  underwear, 53–4
conditioning, 79
conflict, avoiding, 38–9, 73
constipation, 12, 14–15, 32–3
  anal fissures, 15
  causes, 14, 32

Hirschsprung's disease, 13
  refusal to go, 80
  spastic constipation, 15
  treatment, 32–3, 56, 93
control, learning, 71–3
cystitis, 9

D

daycare centres, 55–6, 83
dehydration, 7, 14, 16
nappy rash, 8, 28–9
nappies, 18–27
  at night, 74–5, 76
  changing, 24–7
  disposable nappies, 8, 18–19
  regression, 77
  washable nappies, 8, 20–3
diarrhoea, 13, 15–16, 31
  causes, 15
  food allergy and intolerance, 34
  toddler diarrhoea, 15–16, 56
diet: and constipation, 56, 93
  weaning, 32–3
digestive system, 10–16
disabled children, 90–1
disposable nappies, 8, 18–19, 26–7
distractions, accidents, 83
drinks: before bedtime, 75, 79
  dehydration, 7
  toddler diarrhoea, 16, 56
drying nappies, 22

E

emotional readiness, 38
encopresis, 80
environmental issues, nappies, 23

F

family toilet habits, 59–60
fears, 38, 83
faeces *see* stools
fevers, 7
fibre, 11, 14, 32–3, 93
flushing, 68–9
food allergy and intolerance, 34

G

gastroenteritis, 16
genetics, bed-wetting, 78
germs: hand washing, 69
  hygiene, 68–70
  infections, 9, 16, 30
  sterilizing nappies, 22, 23
  wiping, 67, 69–70
girls: changing nappies, 25
  potty-training, 66–7
glomerulonephritis, 9

H

hand washing, 69
hernias, 13
Hirschsprung's disease, 13
holidays, 48
hygiene, 68–70
hypospadias, 8

I

intensive training, 44
intestines, 11, 13
intussusception, 13, 34

J

journeys, 82–3

K

kidneys, 6, 7
  glomerulonephritis, 9
  infections, 9
kite fold, nappies, 26, 27

L

laundry services, nappies, 22
laxatives, 12, 33
learning difficulties, 90
lifting, 75-6
liners, nappies, 21

M

mattresses, protecting, 75
meconium, 12
medications, bed-wetting, 79
moving house, 47, 48

acknowledgments

A big thank you to Joanne Mackonochie for allowing me to constantly pick her brains, to Mary Dryden for helping with my research, and to Jess Presland and her friends for supplying me with so many potty-training stories. Many thanks also to my editor Tom Broder, for putting so much energy and enthusiasm into my book.

The biggest thank you has to go to my children, Dominic, Lucy and Kate for being my 'guinea pigs' while I was learning these potty-training techniques, and to my husband Robin for his constant and good-natured support.

Alison Mackonochie

Carroll & Brown would like to thank:
Production Karol Davies and Nigel Reed
Computer Support Paul Stradling
Picture Research Sandra Schneider
Photography Jules Selmes

picture credits

1 (left,top right) BabyBjorn (bottom right) The Baby Catalogue; 4 BabyBjorn; 6 Getty Images; 14 Getty Images; 16 Dr Kari Lounatmaa/SPL; 18 Darama/Corbis; 19 Francisco Villaflor/Corbis; 20 Jules Selmes; 21 (centre) JoJo Maman Bebe; 26 Mother and Baby Picture Library/ Dave J Anthony; 27 (top) Mother and Baby Picture Library/Steve Shott; 29 (left) C C Studio/SPL; 31 Jim Varney/SPL; 33 (right) Retna/Sandra Lousada; 34 Jonathan Ashton/SPL; 36 BabyBjorn; 38 BabyBjorn; 39 Getty Images; 41 Mike Bluestone/SPL; 46 Getty Images; 48 Laura Dwight/Corbis; 49 Retna/Sandra Lousada; 50 (top,second from top) BabyBjorn (third from top) The Baby Catalogue (bottom) Mother and Baby Picture Library/Perry Hastings; 51 BabyBjorn; 52 Liane Hentscher/Corbis; 55 Bubbles/Pauline Cutler; 56 Getty Images; 58 Mother and Baby Picture Library/Paul Mitchell; 59 Mother and Baby Picture Library/Ian Hooton; 61 JoJo Maman Bebe; 64 Labat, Jerrican/SPL; 65 Toilet-Time Targets; 66 Mother and Baby Picture Library/ Eddie Lawrence; 67 Bubbles/Jennie Woodcock; 68 Jules Selmes; 72 Mother and Baby Picture Library/Ian Hooton; 74 Powerstock; 77 Jose Luis Pelaez, Inc /Corbis; 80 Mother and Baby Picture Library/Betsie Van Der Meer; 82 (left) Powerstock (right) Mother and Baby Picture Library/Perry Hastings; 83 Ricki Rosen/Corbis Saba; 84 Laura Dwight/Corbis; 86 Rob and Sas/Corbis; 87 Retna/Sandra Lousada; 90 Mother and Baby Picture Library/Ian Hooton; **Front jacket** Getty Images

BabyBjorn
www.babybjorn.com
JoJo Maman Bébé
www.jojomamanbebe.com

The Baby Catalogue
www.thebabycatalogue.com
Toilet-Time Targets
www.toilettimetargets.com